CCAR Journal

The Reform Jewish Quarterly

Contents

From the Editor
At the Gates — בשערים................................. 1

Articles

Symposium: Millennial Engagement
Guest Editors' Introduction............................. 5
Ben Spratt and Joshua Stanton

Legacy Institution and Emergent Community
Innovation in All Generations.......................... 11
Peter J. Rubinstein and Andrew N. Bachman

**Inserting a "Disruptor" into the
   Jewish Spiritual Marketplace**........................ 18
Paul Yedwab

Attending to the Multiplicities 25
Lydia Medwin and Jessica Gross

**Organizational Collaboration and
   Millennial Engagement**............................... 32
Jaclyn F. Cohen and Jason R. Levine

**Investing in Our Infrastructure: Why Congregations
   Matter Now More Than Ever** 41
Aaron Miller

Mind of a Millennial
Millennial Engagement and the Problem of Loneliness...... 48
Marc Katz

CONTENTS

Jewish Millennials and Millennial Judaism 54
Kerry M. Olitzky

**Breast Practices: How a Lactation Support Group
   Taught Me the Possibility of Jewish Community** 61
Amanda Schwartz

**"I Want You to Want Me": A Reflection on the Need
   for Obligation and Covenant** 69
Sara Luria

Finding the Way to Friday 75
Jessica Minnen

Millenni-Y'all: Working with Jews in the South 81
Matthew Dreffin

Israel: A Diaspora Dialogue 88
Hannah Ellenson and Jacqueline Koch Ellenson

MILLENNIAL RESPONSA
The Meaning of Life 97
Amanda Greene and Seth Limmer

Innovative Tradition 104
Kimberly Herzog Cohen and David Stern

Intergenerational Responsa 110
Jeremy Weisblatt and Edwin Goldberg

Millennials, Jewish Values, and Climate Change 114
Jason R. Levine and Ruth A. Zlotnick

BOOK REVIEWS
Siddur Lev Shalem: For Shabbat and Festivals 123
Edward Feld, Senior Editor
Reviewed by Jeffrey Brown

*Eight Questions of Faith: Biblical Challenges that
   Guide and Ground Our Lives* 125
Niles Elliot Goldstein
Reviewed by Peter Knobel

Join the Conversation!

Subscribe Now.

Engage with ideas about Judaism and Jewish life through essays, poetry and book reviews by leading scholars, rabbis, and thinkers.

A Journal for All Jews
The CCAR Journal: The Reform Jewish Quarterly
$125 for one year subscription
$175 for two year subscription

For more information and to order, go to:
www.ccarpress.org or call 212-972-3636 x243
CCAR | 355 Lexington Avenue | New York, NY 10017

At the Gates — בִּשְׁעָרִים

Between Israel and the World

In my career, I have read a handful of essays that have had an enduring impact on my attitude toward Jews and Judaism. One of them is Simon Rawidowicz's "Israel: The Ever-Dying People." Rawidowicz, a scholar in the philosophy of Feuerbach and Krochmal, wrote the essay in 1948, but it did not receive much notice until it was published by his son over fifteen years after his death.

Rawidowicz employed as his starting point, the concluding mishnah of Tractate *Sotah* (9:15), which begins, "When R. Meir died, teachers of homilies were no more . . . ." The mishnah proceeds through a series of *mi-shemet* (when [a revered Sage] died). Each death also brings the demise of some aspect of Jewish culture and learning. The theme of the essay is a familiar one. It can be summed up by the famous quote of Louis XV, "*Apres moi, le deluge.*" Every generation sees themselves as the last.

The perception exists across time and societies. It is especially powerful—and for good reason—among the Jews. After centuries of dispossession, exile, and oppression, Jews have learned to be neither sanguine nor desperate about the future. Rather an anxiety has set in, in which each generation of Jews fear and thus determine not to be the last generation.

The "ever-dying" nature of Israel, Rawidowicz noted, set up a dialectic within Jewish thought; a tug between optimism and pessimism, between hope and fear. One can easily see how the fear of being the last generation is employed in order to place one's hope in the next. Judaism is filled with aphorisms that focus our attention and care on the children. Among the better known is the midrash (*Shir HaShirim Rabbah*) proclaiming that God prefers children to both elders and scholars as guarantors of the Torah.

For me, however, Rawidowicz's most important insight entailed a second dialectic: between Israel and the world. He argued that biblical Israel was fundamentally optimistic about the world; that the arc (or, to use the Hegelian term, the guile) of history bends toward redemption. (Isaiah 2:2: "It shall come to pass in the end of days that the mountain of the Eternal's house shall be the top of the mountains . . . and all nations shall flow unto it.") The experience of the Jews, particularly following the destruction of the second Temple, rather turned Israel inward. The fate of the world was left to messianic judgment, while Jews turned all their hopes and efforts into preserving themselves.

Modernity and emancipation pierced through this self-absorption. In the context of nineteenth-century ideal, Jews could imagine a Messianic Age that did not require divine intervention. This universal messianic hope implied, however, the disappearance of Israel itself. Modernity also occasioned a rise in a virulent anti-Semitism that produced an opposite response: an unforgiving Orthodoxy or a radical Zionism that once more bracketed the world out. Rawidowicz argued that Israel cannot be divided out against the world: "As long as one lives in hell, the other cannot live in paradise."

Attention to the well-being of the next generation of Jews therefore entails attention to the world as well. The future of Israel is dependent upon both continuity and change. Jews must focus intensely on preserving and invigorating Judaism for the next generation. And they must also focus intensely on the living context in which that next generation exists.

With "Israel: The Ever-Dying People" in mind, I am pleased to present this issue's theme: Millennial Engagement. For the sake of survival, the next generation must be engaged, but they are not encountered solely as Jews. They are *Millennials,* a cohort who are defined by social and cultural forces that operate in the larger world beyond the Jewish home or synagogue. We therefore continue to defy our "ever-dying-ness" by focusing on the Jewish guarantors of Torah in the next generation, *and* upon the world in which they live. I am grateful to our colleagues, **Joshua Stanton** and **Ben Spratt**, for developing, organizing, and editing this issue.[1]

Moving On

The Winter issue of each *Reform Jewish Quarterly* is noted by a change in the color of the cover. The variation offers a simple way of dividing sets of the Journal by calendar year. Every other year, the Winter issue also marks a change in the Editorial Board. **Larry Bach, Leah Berkowitz, Dan Fink, Josh Garroway, Jason**

Rosenberg, and **Kinneret Shiryon** have made invaluable contributions to the breadth, depth, and quality of the articles that have been printed in the Journal over the past four years. I am confident that the new Board members—**Yoki Amir, Rachel Sabbath Beit-Halachmi, Oren Hayon, Beth Kalisch, Shira Lander,** and **Brian Stoller**—will carry on with the same attention and diligence exhibited by current and past Board members.

Paul Golomb, Editor

Note

1. One clear mark of a generational shift is to be found in Rabbis Stanton and Spratt's introduction. The preponderance of references and citations are not to be found in hard copy books, but rather in web links.

Symposium: Millennial Engagement

Guest Editors' Introduction

Ben Spratt and Joshua Stanton

The largest generation in American history is coming of age, reshaping nearly every aspect of society. The Millennial generation (approximately 14–36 years of age[1]) is the largest in the labor force,[2] has a spending power of over $200 billion,[3] and is set to inherit $40 trillion in the coming decades.[4] They have grown up during a time of technological change, globalization, and economic disruption and have seldom known stasis in any part of their lives. Perhaps because of this recurrent flux, they are a generation of seekers, pursuing enduring values, meaning, and relationships to sustain them amid such change. They have been slower to marry and move out on their own, and they prioritize access to services over ownership of goods.[5] They want their investment of time, money, and energy to offer a sense of meaning and purpose[6] and are more influenced by the opinions of friends than by brand advertising—and correspondingly want their voices to be heard, as well.[7]

As religious leaders in the United States, we cannot afford to ignore this rising generation. In fact, it is critically important for us to understand Millennials as a generational cohort in order to ensure that our communities endure and thrive in the years ahead. This holds true not only for Millennials themselves, but also insofar as they serve as a bellwether generation and early adopter of technology and social norms that their parents and grandparents soon will utilize as well.

BEN SPRATT (JTS08) is associate rabbi of Congregation Rodeph Sholom and rabbi in residence of Rodeph Sholom School, and is the cofounder of Tribe, a grassroots collaborative of Jewish Millennial engagement in New York City.

JOSHUA STANTON (NY13) is associate rabbi of Congregation B'nai Jeshurun in Short Hills, New Jersey, and is the cofounder of Tribe, a grassroots collaborative of Jewish Millennial engagement in New York City.

Challenges and uncertainties abound in the growing body of research about Millennials, but we must not shy away from them or their possible implications. For example, two data points particularly near to us as rabbis might leave us grasping for easy responses: Millennials both prioritize wellness more than prior generations[8] and are relatively unattached to organized religion. Twenty-nine percent claim no affiliation with any religion, the highest levels of any generation in the last twenty-five years.[9]

Some have suggested that the only explanation is that Millennials are the "self(ie) generation," [10] too narcissistic to grasp the significance of religion and so much else that prior generations hold dear. We maintain that such responses seem callous and lacking in both nuance and empathy. What if Millennials really need ethical, spiritual, and social connection but simply are not finding it in our houses of worship—at least not in the ways that they need? What if our voices are speaking to their needs, but what they really want is to find a way to express their own voices, as well?

In studying this rising generation, religious leaders need courage, compassion, and a willingness to adapt. But if we can summon the strength to listen to Millennials and adapt in authentic ways to the changing demographic landscape, we might even find ourselves living amid an era of spiritual revival.

In his book *After Heaven*, American sociologist Robert Wuthnow articulates decades of research on the trends of religion in America. He notes that most Americans fall into two categories: "dwellers" and "seekers." Those who find meaning and purpose in stability are dwellers. Those who find meaning and purpose in the journey, across shifting landscapes and beyond safe walls, are seekers. Interestingly, within Jewish tradition, we are presented with both modes of meaning. Wuthnow writes:

> [In Judaism, dwelling] spirituality is suggested in stories of the Garden of Eden and of the Promised Land; it consists of temple religion; and it occurs in the time of kings and priests. A spirituality of seeking is tabernacle religion, the faith of pilgrims and sojourners; it clings to the Diaspora and to prophets and judges, rather than to priests and kings. The one inheres to the mighty fortress, the other in desert mystics and itinerant preachers. The one is symbolized by the secure life of the monastery, the cloister, the shtetl; the other by peregrination as a spiritual ideal.[11]

GUEST EDITORS' INTRODUCTION

We are the bearers of two ideals, propelled over and over again in our tradition to leave home only to come home again. We leave a promised land, only to strive to return. Our Patriarchs and Matriarchs enter and leave and enter and leave. We are the wanderers, and we are the builders. We retain the tradition of the Tabernacle, carrying God's presence in the midst of seeking, and we bear the iconic Temple, a fixed house for God. Ours is a perpetual story of leaving in order to return. The challenge is that upon arrival, we never manage to stay put.

Nearly a century ago, the late Rabbi Mordecai Kaplan actualized his vision of the future of the synagogue: the Jewish Center on 86th Street in New York City. Kaplan made this ten-story structure into "a shul with a pool and a school."[12] At that time, he knew that the synagogue had to both create community and help integrate American Jewry into civic life. It needed to become a multifaceted clearinghouse of culture and connection—a truly Jewish Community Center; a social, spiritual, and communal home for them as new immigrants who still felt like outsiders.[13] This model filled the profound needs of the Jewish community at the time.

Now we live at a time of great specialization. Organizations offering meaning in life abound and are designed for this era of seekers: book clubs, Soul Cycle, Pilates studios, meet-up groups, trivia, craft beer making (and drinking) opportunities. This is increasingly becoming true in the Jewish world, as well. If learning is what you want, you can take a class at the Skirball Center at Temple Emanu-El in New York with the top Jewish scholars in the world. If social justice is your calling, the American Jewish World Service will make a bigger impact than the average synagogue. If you want to advocate for Israel, join ARZA or AIPAC or JStreet so that you can remain among those who agree with your political bent. Want to meet a Jewish romantic partner? Try JDate or JSwipe (or countless non-Jewish dating sites on which you can specify a religious persuasion or preference, among other identity markers). Nowadays, wanting your child to become a bar or bat mitzvah is even not reason enough for Jewish institutions to exist. Rooms and rabbis can be rented through a simple search on Google.

Synagogues, and even Jewish Community Centers, which once were the great centers of Jewish meaning, now find themselves surrounded by an array of offerings, each geared with remarkable specificity to the needs and interests of constituents.

The sense of religion as patriotic duty during the Cold War has faded, while the marketplace of meaning has become filled with new options.

For four years, Jewish leadership has been grappling with the mountain of data emerging from the 2013 Pew Study on American Jewish life. There is fascinating information about a wide range of the American Jewish experience, from politics to practices. The most thought-provoking data concerns the decline of synagogue life. Forty years ago, 70 percent of American Jews belonged to a synagogue. Today, that number hovers at only 30 percent. At the same time, as some of our teachers have noted to us, pride in Jewish identity is on the rise, now at 94 percent. This suggests that institutional Jewish affiliation is no longer necessary to affirming Jewishness. The most precipitous declines may be seen in Jewish Millennials.[14] Kaplan's vision for a synagogue as a Jewish intermediary with the broader world worked in a time when Jews could not afford, find access to, or find interest in what secular society offered. Those conditions from a century ago do not exist today. In fact, if Kaplan were alive today, we believe that he would demand a new reconstruction of communal life to fit the needs of American Jewry as it presently exists.

We do not purport to know what institutional changes should take place in order to engage the Millennial generation and reengage other generations and demographic groups that have similarly reduced their participation in organized Jewish life. Though we have cofounded and continue to codirect an empowerment-focused model of Millennial engagement in New York City,[15] we suspect that the American Jewish community has entered a period of much-needed experimentation from which best practices will emerge. This holds true for adaptations by synagogues, Jewish Community Centers, and advocacy organizations—as well as burgeoning new organizations and models. Our hope is not to proclaim victory at having discovered the panacea for our community's demographic challenges—or to suggest that anyone could possibly do so right now—but to convene a conversation that brings together leaders, visionaries, and builders who are actively addressing Millennial engagement within the Jewish community in order to start culling promising principles and practices. This issue of the *Reform Jewish Quarterly* brings together the voices and expertise of many generations of Jewish leaders, all focusing some of their creative energies on Jewish Millennials. All feel the urgency of a changing landscape of Jewish America.

As Andrew Solomon powerfully captures in his book *Far from the Tree*, the formation of identity takes places in two ways. Vertical identities are those attributes and values passed from one generation to the next; horizontal identities are those fostered by one's peer group. Ethnicity and nationality tend to be examples of the former, while genius and sexual identity tend to be examples of the latter. Vertical identities are usually respected as positive traits; horizontal ones (unfortunately) are often minimized or treated as deficits.[16] When horizontal identities are not faced and embraced by the prior generation, the following generation will move far from the tree. In short, our best hope of passing values to the next generation comes from embracing many aspects of identity that Millennials already possess—while sharing in new and meaningful ways Jewish identity markers that we seek to impart.

As the *Mishkan* gave way to *Mikdash* and then in turn to shul, the realities and mind-sets of new generations have continuously called leaders to reenvision the means and modes of Jewish engagement. We hope that this issue of the Journal ignites a larger conversation, as we all encounter with intention this new generation. Studies from every industry and facet of social life indicate that the mentality, priorities, and sense of well-being among Millennials are markedly different—or at least manifested in markedly different ways. The question is what our response to this generation will be.

Notes

1. This precise generational demarcation varies based on sociological study.
2. http://www.pewresearch.org/fact-tank/2015/05/11/millennials-surpass-gen-xers-as-the-largest-generation-in-u-s-labor-force/.
3. http://www.forbes.com/sites/micahsolomon/2015/11/14/2016-is-the-year-of-the-millennial-customer-heres-how-to-be-ready/#61a7d5446e72.
4. http://www.bc.edu/content/dam/files/research_sites/cwp/pdf/Wealth%20Press%20Release%205.28-9.pdf.
5. http://www.goldmansachs.com/our-thinking/pages/millennials/.

6. http://www.gallup.com/reports/189830/millennials-work-live.aspx?utm_source=gbj&utm_medium=copy&utm_campaign=20160615-gbj.
7. http://resources.bazaarvoice.com/rs/bazaarvoice/images/201202_Millennials_whitepaper.pdf.
8. http://www.quirks.com/articles/how-millennials-are-reshaping-health-and-wellness.
9. http://www.pewsocialtrends.org/files/2010/10/millennials-confident-connected-open-to-change.pdf.
10. http://www.nytimes.com/2014/03/08/opinion/blow-the-selfie-generation.html.
11. Robert Wuthnow, *After Heaven: Spirituality in America Since the 1950s* (Berkeley, CA: University of California Press, 1988), 4.
12. Mel Scult, *The Radical American Judaism of Mordecai M. Kaplan* (Bloomington and Indianapolis: Indiana University Press, 2015), 10.
13. http://www.jewishcenter.org/history.html; not to be confused with the Society for the Advancement of Judaism, which Kaplan founded in 1922 as an exploration to new approaches in bringing Judaism into modern American life.
14. http://www.pewforum.org/2013/10/01/chapter-3-jewish-identity/; The number for American Jewry as a whole currently is 31 percent; amongst Reform Jews the number is 34 percent; Conservative Jews, 50 percent; and Orthodox Jews, 69 percent, which indicates the urgency within the Reform world in particular.
15. It is called Tribe, and more information can be found on its website, www.nytribe.com.
16. Andrew Solomon, *Far from the Tree: Parents, Children, and the Search for Identity* (New York: Scribner, 2012), 2, 47.

*Legacy Institution
and Emergent Community*

Innovation in All Generations

Peter J. Rubinstein and Andrew N. Bachman

In a provocative and thoughtful essay published at the beginning of the twentieth century, the writer Jonathan Rosen's *The Talmud and the Internet: A Journey between Worlds* (New York: Farrar, Strauss, & Giroux, 2000) articulated a parallelism between the vast tractates of Rabbinic law and legend and the World Wide Web. Rosen argued that both were worlds in which anything could be found if one simply knew where to look.

This metaphoric framing is a helpful tool for grasping both the innovative nature of our own technological era and the reifying ways in which the Rabbis of the Mishnaic and Talmudic periods reframed study in a post-Temple era in their attempt to sustain Jewish life. Both the Internet today and the foundational texts of Jewish law and lore continue to expand human engagement with the pursuit of knowledge and connect each of us to others across vast distances. In other words, in an increasingly horizontal and global world, we Jews are, perhaps, the original global people. We continue to reinvent our "delivery systems" for knowledge and connection to one another and the Divine even as we maintain our rootedness in the enduring values of Jewish life and civilization. We offer this broad sweep of Jewish history as helpful in making the point.

PETER J. RUBINSTEIN (NY69), Rabbi Emeritus at Central Synagogue in New York City, is Director of Jewish Community at the Bronfman Center for Jewish Life at the 92nd Street Y in New York.

ANDREW N. BACHMAN (NY96) is Founder and President of Water Over the Rocks, an organization dedicated to history, civic responsibility and justice, located in Brooklyn, NY.

During our shared careers teaching in varieties of Jewish communities, in synagogues, JCCs, and Hillels across North America, we have often found that articulating a "big-picture" of Jewish life—its scope, its texts, and traditions; its history and meaning—is an essential first step in exploring with each new generation, now the Millennials, the fundamental question for Jews in modernity: Why be Jewish?

Jews and their partners in the world today face an overabundance of choices regarding who they ought to be. We are born into families; we are educated among a diverse array of peers; we socialize in further diverse groups; and in an age of increasing multiculturalism, our younger generations are defining themselves, as the Pew study has shown, in terms of multiple identities. It ought to be a given, therefore, that the old tried and true way of doing things will not necessarily guarantee Jewish identity and continuity for the next generation. While our communal concern for continuity has been nearly fetishized, best exemplified by any number of new programs that seek to make Judaism and Jewishness "hip" and "relevant," the Jewish people have always been innovating, reframing, and smashing idols in order to continue to sustain an ongoing relationship with one another, with our history, and with our God.

The classical midrash about the patriarch Abraham destroying his father's idols is an object lesson in the ancient Jewish iconoclasm that signifies nascent Judaism's monotheistic break from the idolatrous milieu of the ancient Near East. Echoes of this idea are found in the story of the *Akeidah*, as well, often read as a rejection of the prevalent practice of child sacrifice in the early Bronze Age. In significant ways innovation has been core to our people's story from its earliest references in the Torah.

Abraham and Sarah are fundamentally a family, called upon to become a nation. But that process of transformation from "family" to "nation" is one in which the leaders are considered prophets who talk to the Divine. Only over the course of generations and not until the first diaspora community is born in Egypt are the Israelites defined (by the non-Jewish pharaoh!) as a nation. In fact, until the Exodus, the Rabbis understand all leaders of the Israelites in the Torah to be prophets. After the Exodus, God requires a new institution, the Priesthood, to facilitate a prescribed mode of worship, animal sacrifice, to please the Deity.

This innovation, of priest and prophet in tension and dialogue with one another in order to discern and carry out God's will, holds for several generations until the time of the prophet Samuel. It is then that the people demanded an earthly ruler over Samuel's and God's initial objections. Thus another leadership innovation, kingship, is added to priest and prophet. And so it evolved with Jewish leadership structures until the Babylonian exile in 586 B.C.E.

With the exile to Babylonia, Jewish civilization encountered the political structures of ancient Babylonia and Persia, and ultimately those who returned from exile to the Land of Israel brought with them a more developed institution of Scribe, as articulated in Ezra and Nehemiah. In the period of the Great Assembly, the Keepers and Recorders of the Law laid the groundwork for the incipient Rabbinic era. And though the institutions of priest, prophet, and king endured into the Second Temple period, it is through the agency and the innovation of the Rabbinic class that Judaism flourished and developed. Indeed, it was Yohanan ben Zakkai who negotiated with Rome for Yavneh. The establishment of synagogues and houses of study outside of Jerusalem permitted Judaism and Jewish peoplehood to emerge without a centralized Temple cult of sacrifice and worship. The essence of this critical innovation—the portability of Torah, prayer as a substitute for sacrifice, and the decentralization of leadership—was the seedbed for the next two thousand years of Jewish growth and development.

One can argue that the next chapter in the annals of innovation is found in Maimonides' *Mishneh Torah*, a twelfth-century code of law that sought to consolidate Talmudic law to its essentials, permitting a greater accessibility to the law for students unversed in the complex modes of traditional Talmudic learning. The *Mishneh Torah* evolved to become an indispensable aid in the discernment of Jewish wisdom through the ages.[1]

Perhaps even more influential than the *Mishneh Torah* was the Rambam's *Guide for the Perplexed*, a theological and philosophical work that was addressed to both Torah scholars and those interested in philosophy. Maimonides effectively elevated the pagan philosopher Aristotle to the *beit midrash*, provoking further controversy at the time. But from the perspective of the broad sweep of history, the *Guide* is now an indispensible text for Jewish theological inquiry.

With the Enlightenment and, ultimately, the extension of civil equality to the Jews throughout European communities, our tradition encountered the latest great period of innovation, the tremors of which are still felt to this day. For it was the principles of the Enlightenment that unleashed the process by which Jews could be emancipated and made free as citizens within the countries they resided. Indeed, the French emperor Napoleon reconstituted a "Sanhedrin," which according to the historian Paul Mendes-Flohr was a "messianic" gesture, meant to signify a new era of Jewish history wherein Jews were to practice their faith as loyal citizens of the nations where they lived. No longer a separate and wholly distinct people, Jews would join the family of nations in exchange for their fealty to their adopted homelands. According to Rabbi Dr. David Ellenson, "All Jewish religious leaders, after Emancipation, are constantly compelled to reconcile particular religious tradition with the varied demands of a contemporaneous social and cultural context. With the advent of modernity, Jewish life was transformed in all spheres of social life, and Jewish religious leaders had to mediate between past and present to make Jewish identity a cogent and viable option for Jews in the modern world."[2]

In relatively short order, emancipation and modernity both unleash the innovations of denominationalism thereby creating Reform, Conservative, Orthodox, and Reconstructionist Judaism, as well as movements for Jewish nationalism in the form of Zionism and Jewish socialist movements of the nineteenth and twentieth centuries. Zionism represented a counter-messianic movement that eschewed waiting for the Messiah in favor of a Jewish national home in the Land of Israel claimed by historical right and international diplomacy. The movement for Jewish socialism (independent of socialist strands within the Zionist Movement) was decimated by the World Wars and anti-Semitism of the Soviet Union.

Dr. Ellenson's words ring true especially in our American context, which is defined by freedom of choice and expression, along with multiple identities and rapid decision-making enabled by ongoing technological advance. Our mandate as leaders is to create environments in which Jews can "mediate between past and present" in order to make "cogent and viable" choices in what it means to be Jewish today.

From the rise of the independent minyanim to synagogues without walls; from small groups inside synagogues to service learning fellowships committed to social justice; and from arts and culture festivals to podcasts and Jewishly identified pop culture content delivery like *Curb Your Enthusiasm*, *Transparent*, and *Broad City*, there are a seemingly infinite number of ways to identify with and connect to being Jewish.

At the 92nd Street Y, New York's oldest Jewish cultural institution, we are reinventing ways to connect with Jewish culture and values. For example, by recognizing that a pathway into Jewish life is often through our children, 92Y's Shababa program offers Jewish learning through song, puppetry, theater, and community-building for thousands across the country. With the help of an Innovation Team, we did this by scaling our values and expanding programs like 92Y Shababa to other communities through the Shababa Network, a national initiative that we are now introducing to Christian and Muslim leaders in the city in order to share our methodology for bringing community and meaning to those who seek it.

Harnessing the power of Facebook Live, we have convened Shabbat discussions, visited important civil rights sites in the South for an exploration of the historic Black-Jewish alliance, and honored important figures from Jewish history by visiting their graves in cemeteries around New York City. Gathering small groups of young Jews responsible for Jewish-focused startups, we explored possible collaborations with the Y. This coming year we will have a live chat component as part of our live streaming of our High Holy Days services. It will be convened and facilitated by our "digital rabbi," a student at HUC-JIR who joins a newly appointed innovation fellow, who is also a rabbinical student at HUC-JIR. Rather than interning at a congregation, this student chose to spend his year in fulfillment of his internship requirement learning how diverse community centers, which offer a vast array of programming to Jews and non-Jews, are now at the forefront of Jewish service and connection throughout the United States.

Perhaps unimaginable a generation ago, our ability to train rabbinical students today in this methodology is made possible, in part, by the Be Wise Fellowship in Jewish Entrepreneurialism at HUC-JIR, where Peter serves as the program coordinator. The Be Wise Fellowship in Jewish Entrepreneurialism provides an opportunity for students to explore our history and to further Rabbi Stephen Wise's legacy by conceptualizing and carrying out bold and creative initiatives that respond to the needs of contemporary Jewry, precisely the demographic of young Jews that the Y and countless other Jewish organizations seek to connect to Jewish life today.

In addition to traditional learning, basic Judaism and text-based courses, we are also developing new classes, talks, and salon-style discussions on Jewish values in today's world. We bring the global Jewish community to technology through initiatives like the #NewYearPrayer, which draws people together from all over the world resulting in 2.2 million people reached on social media in 2015; #GivingTuesday (which follows Black Friday, Small Business Saturday, and Cyber Monday) underscores the Jewish vision of *tzedakah* during the high season of commercialism; and the moral audit Givingpause.org, which measures personal behavior against self-perceived values. Whether one is searching for tradition, inspiration, or something new, 92Y is creating meaningful new ways to help Millennials and others connect with Jewish culture, heritage, values, and wisdom in a way that works for the individual seeker.

Peter tells the story that on the way to 5776 Rosh HaShanah Eve services his tech-savvy wife poked him and said, "It's at 9,000!" Knowing she didn't mean the stock market, he asked her what was at 9,000. "It's that video about Rosh HaShanah—a reflection about what it means and why it matters—that you filmed in our apartment . . . More than 9,000 people have viewed it!" This was when we began to comprehend the revolutionary impact that the 92nd Street Y and we could have together in shaping Jewish life globally. The enthusiastic response to the video suggested the difference we could make in enhancing knowledge, identity, and involvement among Jews who might not otherwise be connected to their heritage.

The Rosh HaShanah reflection eventually received more than 115,000 views. And the Global Blessing we launched from 92Y was passed by 14 communities—synagogues and Jewish community centers—from Australia to Hawaii. We believe it was the first time in history that Jewish people worldwide celebrated Rosh HaShanah in unison, embodying the Talmudic aspiration that all Jews are responsible for and linked to each other. In 2016, moreover, the New Year Song commissioned and produced by the Y received over 6 million views.

A look back over the archives of the past one hundred years here at the 92nd Street Y shows us that in each generation, our forebears responded to the exigencies of their own age with the unique Jewish voices of their time. From the wave of refugees who came to New York between 1880 and 1920, who needed training in acculturation and American citizenship; the rise of labor and civil rights; the crisis of refugees as Europe lurched toward war not once but twice in a thirty-year span; the utter devastation of European Jewry in the Holocaust; the creation of the state of Israel; the rescue of Soviet and Ethiopian Jewry—all were front and center of the 92Y's own deliberations and actions for what it meant to be a Jew in today's world.

And so it is in our own day. Crises abound; communities are seemingly separated by vast distances yet remarkably held close together by the intimacy of technology's most hospitable manifestations. It is our contention that by embracing innovation, using the tools at our disposal and daring even to fail, our growth and sustenance as a people will be sustained openness, experimentation, and the adventure of original invention so that together we can wrestle with the most searing issues confronting us as Jews and as world citizens.

Notes

1. It should be noted that the *Mishneh Torah* created controversy in its own day due to the Rambam's decision not to include sources for his legal decisions along with the fear that this abbreviated version of law would discourage in-depth study.
2. David Ellenson, *After Emancipation: Jewish Religious Responses to Modernity* (Cincinnati: HUC Press, 2004).

Inserting a "Disruptor" into the Jewish Spiritual Marketplace

Paul Yedwab

I am often regaled by native Detroiters with childhood memories of joyous holiday shopping excursions downtown to the resplendent Hudson's Department Store. Unfortunately, by the time I arrived, that iconic building was a mere shell, but Hudson's was still the anchor at most of our suburban shopping malls. Then suddenly, Hudson's disappeared, seemingly into thin air. As it turns out, however, the Dayton Hudson Corporation did not go away. Instead, Hudson's had inserted into the market its own competitor, creating what is known in the business world as a "disruptor." You've probably heard of that small startup; it is called Target. Eventually, the disruptor grew to become the second largest discount retailer in the world, overtaking its parent company to the point where the mall stores were sold off and the name of the corporation changed. This strategy of a large corporation planting its own competition or disruptor into the marketplace is one that is having a great deal of success of late. Of course, the new entity does not generally eclipse its parent company as in the case of Hudson's. More often, it is just a way of putting a hipper, cooler, groovier spin on the organization's core business in order to reach people that the more established entity cannot, while at the same time sending out feelers as to where the market may be headed in the future.[1]

What the Pew and other subsequent reports have shown quite clearly is that this new generation of Millennials is membership-phobic, dues-resistant, and organization-wary. And the question we have all been asking since is "How are we, as an organized

---

PAUL YEDWAB (NY86) is the rabbi of Temple Israel in West Bloomfield, Michigan, and the author of six books on Jewish learning.

Jewish community, to attract this new breed of 'consumer' to our old Jewish watering holes?" Our answer, here at Temple Israel of Metropolitan Detroit, was to dig a new "Well." Inspired by a dynamic future planning committee, supported by a forward-thinking executive and temple board, and funded by a visionary philanthropist, we decided to meet this stubbornly under-affiliated cohort exactly where they are, to reach beyond the walls of our own "spiritual fortress," if you will, by inserting a "disruptor" into the local Jewish marketplace; a disruptor known as The Well.

What distinguishes The Well from the other outstanding Millennial outreach programs that have been established by congregations nationwide is that The Well is an independent entity—a disruptor to the synagogue movement rather than a branch of it. Although always identified as "a project of the Lori Talsky Zekelman Fund at Temple Israel," and strongly supported by the synagogue through open access to our accounting, graphics, and administrative departments, The Well is independently branded, with its own website (www.meetyouatthewell.org), stationery, and budget. While technically an employee of the temple, The Well's founding director, Rabbi Dan Horwitz, recently named as one of the *Forward*'s "most inspiring rabbis," is free of any formal pulpit responsibilities whatsoever. His portfolio is solely to build and grow The Well and to weave interpersonal networks with the under-affiliated community-wide. Dan's success is not measured by how many people join the shul but rather by how many Jewish souls he touches.

In biblical times, the well was a place to gather, to conduct business, to meet one's spouse, and to schmooze. Yet the waters of the well were not contained within its walls; they flowed naturally beyond any boundaries. So it is with programming and outreach of our Well.

This, however, begs the question: What will this do for the temple? Frankly, we have no idea. Our calculation is that if we can motivate young Jewish adults to value being part of a Jewish community now, then there is a better chance that, when the time comes for them to raise a family, they will seek out a temple and perhaps that temple will be our temple.

Why is this type of outreach so important for us as liberal Jews? Last year I was invited to attend the *Kinus HaShluchim* of the

Chabad Movement. I happened to meet a young Chabad rabbi who had been given two years' salary to go create a Jewish community in Ghana—and then went ahead and did it! "If our 'competition' can do that in Africa," I thought to myself, "why can't Reform Judaism do that here in North America?"

To give credit where credit is due, however, I must mention that this question was first posed by my father, Rabbi Stanley Yedwab, many years ago when he urged his childhood pal, then HUC-JIR president, Rabbi Fred Gottschalk z"l, to create a rabbinic service program that would allow newly ordained rabbis to pay off their student loans by committing to work for two years launching new congregations in urban environments. In essence, he was advocating for the creation of a Reform version of Chabad. The project never got off the ground for financial reasons, but we are able to advance the core concept through our efforts with The Well: to bring a liberal rabbinic voice to the Chabad methodology. And what is that methodology? Engage first, then worry about affiliation and solicitation later.

So far, the success of this new approach has been astounding. In this inaugural season, Rabbi Dan has held over 200 one-on-one coffees with members of our target population and, along with his amazing wife, Miriam (who not surprisingly perhaps came up with the name of The Well), has welcomed young adults to their home for virtually every Shabbat and holiday dinner. Programming-wise, The Well's more than 70 gatherings have drawn over 1,000 unique participants, with well over 2,000 in total attendance. When you consider that Metro Detroit has perhaps 5,000 Jewish Millennials out of a total Jewish population of only 60,000, it is a remarkable ratio.

Here is just a small sampling of the programs that The Well has sponsored in its first year:

- A campaign that challenged Jews worldwide to take time each day in the month leading up to the High Holy Days to introspect and then post their feelings on Facebook.
- A communal *Tashlich* event that drew five hundred people to the heart of the city in order to cast their sins into the Detroit River.
- Eight straight days of gatherings in the Horwitz backyard sukkah, built by volunteers out of reclaimed doors from the

city of Detroit and decorated in tribute to the Heidelberg Project.
- Monthly text-study programs held in cool venues that regularly reach up to 150 participants, without using alcohol as a draw. One recent example was an event focused on LGBTQ issues, held very intentionally at the Holocaust Memorial Center, featuring Judge Bernard Friedman discussing his federal court ruling opening the doors for gay marriage nationwide.
- The initiation of multiple shared interest networks, ranging from a women's Rosh Chodesh gathering, to a men's whiskey group, to a Shabbat dinner club, to a giving circle.
- A "Nice Jewish Boy/Nice Jewish Girl of the Month" feature in its newsletter highlighting amazing (and eligible!) local singles.
- "Big Idea Breakfasts," where folks come together to discuss the big issues of the day before heading off to work.
- Family events, such as Shabbat picnics and Tot Shabbat sing-alongs in the city.
- A Torah and Tailgate in Ann Arbor, Jewish music jam sessions, a dress-in-white garden party for Tu B'Av, a program called "Let's Have Dinner and Talk about Death," Kabbalah yoga, a Shabbat camping trip, and Shabbat experiences for young adults held down in Detroit, not far from where that old Hudson's building used to stand.

So, what wisdom have we gleaned from our first year of engaging Millennials? According to our disruptor-in-chief, Rabbi Dan Horwitz, we have learned that:

- Young adults are definitely interested in having a personal relationship with a rabbi! The caveat is that the rabbi must speak their language, meet them where they are, and eliminate the bureaucracy often associated with congregational life. Of course, so many of our movement's rabbis already do approach Millennials in this open manner. What we may not realize, however, is that something as simple as making an appointment to see the rabbi through her/his administrative assistant may be an obstacle to this new generation more accustomed to simply dropping a text or Facebook message.

- It is clear that Millennials crave the opportunity to take an active role in shaping Jewish experiences for themselves and others. It takes more time and energy to engage a host committee of young adults than simply to plan the program ourselves, but if the goal is to engage and connect, it is the best path in outreach. When Millennials are excited about what they are doing, they will use their own social media and personal contacts to reach out to their friends, who will inevitably support them by attending or donating.
- With Jewish Millennials frequently marrying in their early thirties and waiting to begin their families, there can be a two-decade gap or more between the time they leave our religious school programs and the time they might turn to a synagogue in order to obtain a Jewish education for their own children. Therefore, the issue of "membership" may be a red herring. Instead our goal must be to fill that affiliation gap with Jewish meaning. From that meaning, affiliation will eventually arise.
- Millennials are most definitely open to the idea of having "skin in the game," and the recent tendency of the Jewish community to offer everything for free only infantilizes them. These young adults can and will contribute, if not robustly in the form of dues or fees at first, then at the very least through the bringing of potluck dishes, program supplies, or gifts to be donated to local shelters. That is not to say that these outreach programs will be self-sustaining. As I am fond of saying, "No transformational Jewish organization in the twenty-first century will thrive on dues and fees alone." Visionary philanthropists are an important key to success. But if the meta-curriculum is that Jewish involvement has no cost whatsoever, what will become of our Jewish institutions when those brought up in that world are ready to take their place at the helm?

While it is true that Detroit does enjoy a relatively cohesive Jewish community, it is also true that the market "penetration" The Well has achieved in a very short period is noteworthy. We wonder what we could achieve as a movement if other mainstream liberal congregations (or collections of congregations) inserted disruptors into their own local spiritual marketplaces.

Admittedly, there are challenges that this new model has yet to fully overcome and it is important that we explicate them here:

- We are not yet sure what a sustainable funding structure for this type of endeavor will look like in the future. After all, many of the successful startup spiritual communities garnishing well-deserved national focus are able to pay their bills through the offering of bar/bat mitzvah and other life-cycle ceremonies. In contrast, The Well very intentionally eschews offering such traditional synagogue services since its overriding goal is to eventually mainstream young adults into the established Jewish communal structures. So, although we have been quite successful in engaging both philanthropists and Millennial participants thus far, we have yet to establish a steady and reliable income stream that will take us beyond our initial four-year pilot grant.
- The Well has already received a generous foundation grant to expand its programming staff and that is extremely exciting. We are highly cognizant, however, of the "bureaucratization" that sometimes accompanies rampant growth.
- The boundary line The Well must walk with regard to its affiliation with a mainstream temple is a fine one indeed. Very understandably, the temple's leadership wants to ensure that The Well's good works are associated with the shul that founded and continues to support it. On the other hand, the core tasks of attracting both Millennial participants and foundation contributors sometimes demand that The Well retain its distance. So far, due to an exceptionally forward-thinking lay leadership, we have walked this line quite successfully, but it is an issue that must be tended carefully and continually.

With all of those caveats in mind, however, I will conclude with an exhortation: this is a time to be daring! We are engaged in nothing less than an existential struggle to sustain and strengthen liberal Judaism in the face of increasingly aggressive competitors, creeping disaffection, and a growing disconnect between our existent communal structures and the needs of this next generation. So here is our invitation: If you are interested in digging a "Well" in your own backyard, please do not hesitate to contact us for, as we say here in Detroit, we'd love to "meet you at The Well."

Note

1. For more on the "disruptor" phenomenon and the Hudson's story in particular, please see Dan Libenson's June 2016 webinar in the Alliance for Continuing Rabbinic Education's series, http://allianceforcre.org/.

Attending to the Multiplicities

Lydia Medwin and Jessica Gross

It was one of those moments when you think to yourself: How did I get here? And yet, here I was, standing on a balcony in Malibu, overlooking the sun setting over the Pacific, as we concluded the wedding of an African American Catholic groom to his Russian American Jewish bride with a jump over a broom and a crushing of the glass. And on the surface, it does seem pretty unlikely, radical even, this unconventional Jewish wedding. Yet, any of us who have worked with Millennials in any capacity know that, if there is one thing we can definitively say about Millennials, it is that there is nothing we can definitively say about Millennials. The very thing that defines this generation is their multiplicity of identities, ideologies, interests, and needs. Whether or not we clergy or Jewish professionals feel comfortable with this melding of identities and this multiplicity of interests and needs, it is clear that Millennials absolutely do. If we as a Jewish community are interested in engaging Millennials, both within our established organizations and outside of them, we must be able to meet them in a multiplicity of ways. And the only way to do THAT is figure out how to lash our various organizations together, to weave together the leaders, groups, and institutions that serve Millennials in all their different ways. If we can do this, young Jews will see that they can continue to be the individuals that they are while also attending to the community that they need.

We are two rabbis. Lydia works in a synagogue, Jessy works everywhere but (sort of). We have continually come back to the same realization from our two distinct vantage points: there are

---

LYDIA MEDWIN, MAJE, (LA10) is Director of Community Engagement and Outreach for The Temple Hebrew Benevolent Congregation of Atlanta, GA.

JESSICA GROSS, MAJE, (LA12) is Director of Charm City Pride, an outreach of the Jewish Community Center of Greater Baltimore to people in their 20s and 30s.

so many great things happening to ignite Millennial Jews, but we need to connect and network them in order to create a cohesive Jewish journey, more than just an episode. Emerging adults should be able to transition from college to career (or graduate school) to family life (or not) to vibrant peer group to extended synagogue community—across cities or even countries. We cannot do so as organizations or leaders who act alone.

It reminds us of one juicy anecdote about how a rabbi can build bridges across geographic and chronological expanses for the Millennials they serve. One day, in a coffee shop, a young woman overheard Jessy speaking with another woman about to embark on a yearlong program to Israel. The young woman chimed in sharing that she had just returned from one, and when Jessy was finished with her scheduled meeting she went to learn more about the young woman's experience living in Israel. In five minutes, the two connected the dots of who they knew in common vis-à-vis friendships and summer camps, and Jessy invited the young woman to show up at a Charm City Tribe[1] event, a community effort for people in their twenties and thirties looking to tap into Jewish culture and tradition in downtown Baltimore (a group Jessy founded and directs). The woman became a regular participant, and when she decided to follow her twin sister to Chicago, she sought out Jessy to ask, "What's the Charm City Tribe of Chicago . . . and who is gonna be my rabbi?" Jessy told her of a community she felt would be a good fit, introduced her to the rabbi, and made sure to prep her for the ways in which her experiences were likely to mirror those in Baltimore while also being clear that the community in Chicago felt more like a synagogue than Charm City Tribe. When the young woman returned for a visit, she met Jessy for coffee and shared with her the experiences of tapping into the Jewish community in her new city. She shared her experiences of becoming a regular participant in the community and how she "[goes] to shul twice a month which [she] hasn't done [her] whole life!"

Another anecdote we love comes from The Temple, in Atlanta, where Lydia is the Director of Congregational Engagement and Outreach. She and others on her staff hold weekly "office hours," during which time any guest is welcome to come tour The Temple and learn about the community. At the same time, Temple staff, working with the engagement principle of using every encounter to build the relationship, also seek to learn about the guest. It's called "Fridays at Four." During one of these Fridays at Four, a recent graduate from University of Georgia at Athens came to speak with us to learn more about how to get involved. Having grown up in rural Georgia, she felt lost in Atlanta and came to The Temple to find a circle of new friends. After learning about The Well, The Temple's young adult community, and the 50+ small groups covering a variety of affinities and neigborhoods, in addition to our commitment to social justice work,[2] she decided to give The Temple a try. She was then welcomed by the Roshim (lay leaders in the same demographic, whose roles are to program engagement opportunities for their peers as well as welcome all new members) and they invited her to come to their next event, The Women of the Well. When she showed up to that event, she was welcomed by her 4 new friends and had a couple more friends by the end of the evening. At subsequent events, she always knew she'd see a friend, and those relationships continue to deepen today. She thanks us every turn for the gift of helping her find "her tribe."

These stories are the exception to the rule. We don't currently have the language or structures to help facilitate this kind of bridging. It happens on a case-by-case basis, when a person tells their rabbi or community leader, "Hey, I'm headed this way" and that leader is thoughtful enough to think about who he/she knows that would "catch" them in their new place. Or when a young professional is hungry enough for Jewish experiences that they come on their own. This is not to say that there aren't rich networks within our individual communities and around the country doing really interesting things. But these kinds of connections cannot be made on a community-wide basis unless we create this structure first.

In the cases cited above, as in many others, the focus needs to be on the individual and on their relational connections. Our success as a collective depends on our accomplishments with individuals and the relationships we build with them. But our focus cannot stop there, but must also extend to helping them build relationships with one another as leaders and across organizations.

There are so many opportunities when we think about creating these bridges for young adults, and just as many challenges. For one: place and space. Jessy likens Charm City Tribe to the model of a food truck. Charm City Tribe brings a consistent menu of options, flavor, and style to every place they go, despite popping up in a variety of places, at various times as the calendar and opportunities present moments in which to do so. In that way, not being limited to a brick-and-mortar space helps us to pop up Judaism and facilitate Jewish connect points with people in all the places they normally go. They seek to create "Jacob wrestling with the Angel" moments; popping up in a place that people may come to regularly—a brewery, an art gallery, a music venue—but according to the rhythm of the Jewish holiday cycle, and they transform an otherwise familiar space to help to mark Jewish time and bring Jewish experience alive. It is the hope that participants will stop at some point and say, "Wow, I've been here a hundred times but something is different and I feel connected in a way I didn't realize I could . . . I think I'll show up for the next holiday." It's a great opportunity to be outside the walls of Jewish places where a lot of this generation does not routinely go and to pop up inside of places where they do go, and in doing so, transform the purpose of their being there for Jewish meaning-making and connections.

Still, the "pack in/pack out" model of having to bring everything you need to effectively make an experience happen is something that takes much more time and attention to do than in spaces that serve up Jewish experiences on an ongoing basis. The opportunity to create a sense of connection to an actual place is virtually nonexistent. People don't return to the same place over time in ways that might start to feel like home. At least, not a Jewish home. It is not a place where they come to associate a physical location with the purposes of participating in and learning more about what it means to be Jewish, and while we joke about the "pack in/pack out" model, it is a real factor in man/woman power, bandwidth, and the need to DIY in almost every sense of the word.

This is a strength in which synagogues can be highly functional; when done well, a synagogue can feel like home and community members can take for granted that all the program's supplies will be ready and accessible. This allows synagogues to offer a greater number of opportunities for gathering and, if the architecture and design intentionally allow for it, a place of retreat and sociability.

Another limitation is the ability to go deeper. It's true there are small segments of the Charm City Tribe population who have taken their Jewish participation offline in the moments in between organized gatherings to strengthen relationships and participate in Jewish experience. But it is also true that while Charm City Tribe can turn out five hundred people for a Chanukah party, it takes more effort to get ten to fifteen people together to learn on a regular basis than it does to turn out hundreds for a onetime, socially forward, event. Engagement is a process and Charm City Tribe does a great job at being a first step along the way, but it is by no means the endgame.

If the endgame is deep commitment to Jewish community and expanded Jewish knowledge and meaning-making, we might now return our focus to synagogues. Synagogues can offer a greater breadth of Jewish experiences than the independent community generally can, and often with a greater sense of continuity and depth. At The Temple, community members are presented the chance to commit one of 53 Temple Connect small groups, a lay-led group of eight to twelve people who meet monthly around a shared interest or need. Each group member agrees to a group *b'rit* such that they understand that their presence is an investment in the others in their group. These group members learn Jewish texts together, derive greater meaning from their daily lives together, and understand new relevance to their Jewish community together. They also realize how much they matter to one another and to the community as individuals, by bringing their most authentic selves and their highly-valued intrinsic gifts. While not all these groups were not designed specifically to serve our Millennials, these young Jews do join Temple Connect groups, either as their group's leader, as a part of generationally diverse groups, and as part of Millennial-specific groups as well.

But synagogues are far less able to "meet Millennials where they are" and tend towards slower evolution and responsiveness. In addition, each synagogue offers different strengths and foci with regards to prayer, social justice, commitment to Israel, and more. How would a commitment-shy Millennial know which synagogue might speak to them? Moreover, what rabbi will they entrust to guide their spiritual journey, and what community will they find that reflects the people and values they are looking for outside those walls as well? Whose responsibility is it to help them find their home? And whose responsibility is it to push back on the often-cited Millennial focus on "Me" as opposed to "Us?" These questions are crucial to address as we raise our intention about building the bridge from both sides.

This construction effort brings to light the last area worth considering in this phase: perception. Jessy is often asked, "Why can't there be more rabbis like you?" And she always responds, "There is a whole generation of us and we are everywhere!" Between our training at the Hebrew Union College and its approach employed to grow cohorts of rabbis who would be relevant change-makers, we can confidently say that there are many others out there with similar mentalities, methodologies, and approaches—and many of them are inside synagogues!

If they were in the same city, Jessy could surely set up a system to help build bridges to the work Lydia is doing at The Temple in Atlanta, where Lydia and her colleagues are working on engaging current synagogue members and those outside their walls. The Temple engages hundreds of young professionals in the course of a year, eighty of whom regularly attend monthly Shabbat services called The Well. They are building micro-communities, an attempt to individualize the experience of each congregant. The clergy and staff are hip and vibrant and excited to be changing the culture of Atlanta's oldest and largest Jewish congregation. Lydia will often say, "We believe our work will keep members engaged in deep, substantive, and meaningful ways over the course of many years, but how will our young professionals find out about these authentic and meaningful relationships to Judaism, God, and one another when there is such an allergy to Jewish organizational affiliation and membership?"

Bringing unengaged and unaffiliated Millennials into some organized Jewish space is like crossing a sizable river. On the one side are the leaders, federation execs, and rabbis who want to be of service to these young adults and current leaders who depend on what drew them in as a model for what they think ought to draw in leaders on the rise. On the other side are the young adults who have just started their Jewish journeys outside of any major institution and are committed to the pace and trends that define their generation and they expect will define the activities and affinity groups to which they align themselves. If they are going to cross the proverbial river to the "other side" where rooted Jewish community stands, we need to find a series of rocks sturdy enough to stand on each step of the way to bridge their journey. And we need to allow them to stand long enough to get their footing in that place in order to anticipate their next step, and even the authority and space to shape that foothold to meet their needs.

So often, we rush our people through the steps. They show up to one event and then we send them membership information or a pledge card and they turn around and walk right back out the door. It is critical to bring our next generation of unengaged folks into our communal spaces, but we need to honor the time and attention it takes every step along the journey; indeed to give that time and attention to make sure it unfolds in a way that compels them to want to take the next step towards deeper commitment. And we need to make space for creative conversations between these various leaders and institutions so that a new paradigm might grow to meet the younger generations halfway.

We face an incredible challenge in our leadership, but draw tremendous inspiration from the notion that our task is no different than that of every generation who came before us: to pass Jewish tradition onto the next generation with enough integrity and authenticity to link to where it has come from and with enough relevance and approachability that the newer generation sees the timeless and ever relevant kernels of wisdom it possesses. Grounded in hope with a healthy dose of realism, we believe the Judaism of the future is in good hands. It will require our work to construct these networks and bridges, to learn how to cross them with excitement for what is on the other side, and to not be afraid as we move forward.

Notes

1. Charm City Tribe is a community effort for people in their twenties and thirties looking to tap into Jewish tradition and culture in creative and meaningful ways. Through large-scale community events that tap into the rhythm of the Jewish calendar (Mobile Sukkah, Hannukah BrewHaHa, Wild Purim Rumpus), ongoing monthly Schmooze and Brews and Shabbat Pot Luck dinners and a community connector model that builds one-on-one relationships, Charm City Tribe serves as a clearinghouse for people looking to tap into Jewish life in a variety of ways.
2. I extend appreciation to my colleagues at The Temple—Rabbis Berg, Spinrad, and Lapidus and Engagement Associate Summer Jacobs—for their creaqtive work and partnership in all of these areas and more.

Organizational Collaboration and Millennial Engagement

Jaclyn F. Cohen and Jason R. Levine

Introduction

What comes to mind when you think of Seattle? For many, it's coffee, rain, the Space Needle, and fish throwers at Pike Place Market. What probably wouldn't immediately come to mind—and, indeed it did not register with either of us back when we were fortunate to be offered rabbinic positions here—was Seattle's unprecedented Jewish communal growth. This city in the far northwest corner of the United States has seen a 70 percent increase in its Jewish population in the last thirteen years.[1] A booming economy continues to draw thousands to the region each month—many of them to work for Amazon, Microsoft, Starbucks, and Boeing, among others. Many are Jews of every color, denomination, and background; Jews in their twenties, thirties, and early forties, who have been recruited from leading colleges and graduate school programs from around the country and beyond.

Rapid population growth presents tremendous opportunities and unique challenges for any city. It has certainly been true of Seattle and, more broadly, the Puget Sound region. This is especially true of this area's religious communities. Washington State is consistently identified nationally as fertile ground for the "nones," who do not identify with any religious community. In fact, fully one-third of Seattleites identify as "nones." We are tied

---

JACLYN F. COHEN (LA14) is a rabbi at Temple De Hirsch Sinai in Seattle and Bellevue, Washington, and serves as rabbinic liaison to the Temple's outreach to area Jews in their twenties and thirties, The Tribe.

JASON R. LEVINE (C13) is the Associate Rabbi of Temple Beth Am in Seattle, Washington, where he oversees youth engagement within the congregational community.

in our "none-ness" with San Francisco and only second to our neighbor to the south, Portland.[2] Simply put, we are a top destination for those who consider themselves unaffiliated, assimilated, or disconnected—including the self-identified "spiritual-but-not-religious" crowd. This extends far beyond Jewish circles: churches, mosques, and religious community centers largely struggle within this same milieu.

The reaction of greater Seattle's Jewish organizations and institutions is probably what one might expect in such a situation. Different groups have sought to engage similar niches of the population. As the community has grown, so have the number of organizations and institutions actively engaged with the Jewish community. Yet these various groups continued to work independently. Indeed, like so many other North American cities that have a range of institutions working to serve the same population, we who serve Seattle's Jewish community often find ourselves working parallel to others doing similar, if not identical, work. In that type of environment, a competitive, scarce-resources mentality could dominate.

Yet, within the specific niche of Seattle young adult engagement, there has emerged a powerful model for what is possible when organizations choose to look at one another as collaborators rather than competitors, as allies and fellows instead of opponents and rivals. Our model—the Engager Network—has been able to accomplish something meaningful within the most Jewishly unidentified age group.[3] Most importantly, it has managed to inspire and motivate a small group of Jewish professionals so that we can, in turn, create something inspiring and worthwhile for the next generation of involved, passionate, connected Jews.

History and Formation

In the summer of 2014, leaders from Birthright: Next[4] convened an "Engager Network," a term coined by the Jim Joseph Foundation. Its directive was to connect professionals and lay leaders responsible for Jewish Millennial engagement and programming. The goals of the group were fourfold:

- Increasing trust, mutual respect, and transparency among local engagers

- Accelerating knowledge, skill-sharing, collaborations, and connectional intelligence
- Diving deep into the nuances and needs of Jewish Millennials and engagement issues
- Serving as local platforms for professional development and peer mentoring and support[5]

The staff of Hillel at the University of Washington—then-Jconnect[6] Director Elise Peizner and Director of Strategy Josh Furman—first arranged for representatives of Seattle's various young adult groups to come together one evening for nosh and discussion. The context offered was, "Let's gather together for post-Birthright follow-up and general networking." Neither one of us was present at that meeting, but we each received similar, disappointing feedback: those present weren't sure what they were doing there. The largest presence in the room, Jconnect itself, was seen as dominating the conversation because they had so much to offer. Quite simply, the conversation stalled as quickly as it started and left quite the awkward impression.

It took about ten months before Jconnect convened the group once again—only this time the "call to action" was different. First, the only people included were professionals—this, to a certain degree, leveled the playing field of organizational knowledge. It also created a safe space for us to communicate with one another separate from our constituents.

Second, there was a clear, thoughtful agenda proposed by Elise Peizner. Knowing that Jconnect would still be perceived as having the largest presence and the most to contribute, Peizner proposed topics that would offer common ground for all organizations and professionals present. Among those topics were these universal questions:

- What does it mean to work as partners in young adult engagement?
- What does it mean to be co-sponsors of each other's events?
- How can we communicate most effectively with one another and as a community?
- What are our goals for this specific network?
- How can we best serve one another, challenge one another to grow, and support one another?[7]

This was a tremendous act of redirection and humility on Peizner's and Jconnect's part, as well as a clear recognition that we all had something to offer and something to learn. Instead of the largest group in town dominating the discussion, Jconnect created space for all others to share, built a level playing field for all to succeed, and planted the seeds to develop a united community.

Finally, we decided that in order to create a consistent and lasting model, each meeting would be hosted in rotation at our various organizations. Through this, no one group "owned" or dominated the whole. It was, for many of us, a clear statement of collective ownership and participation. The foundational principles of this group were clear, and all felt heard. From that moment onward, the Engager Network truly began to form.

Our Work Together

Our next meeting within this new structure took place in the spring of 2015. The primary goal was to shine a spotlight on ourselves and the organizations we serve. We created a chart featuring all the groups at the table and compiled the following information for each group:

- Name of organization/group
- Our target audience
- Where we're most successful
- What the community perceives is our greatest strength
- Where we'd like to grow

Together we methodically and eagerly analyzed our own work and were able to offer thoughtful feedback to others. It may sound overly simplistic or basic, but this was truly the first time any of us had ever participated in an exercise like this. Every group had great power. Every organization had a unique mission. Every group contributed something meaningful to the larger Seattle Jewish community. There was space for all, whether it was a focus on smaller segments of the wide Millennial age range, such as immediately post-college or young families; groups that represented the range of Jewish ritual and practice; geographic distribution reaching out to all parts of town; or a programmatic attention on social justice, culture, nature, text study, and more. It was refreshing, insightful, and it brought us to the collective realization that we each had something valuable to offer.

We continue to meet regularly every four to six weeks. Our meetings begin with a text study led by the host and continue with a discussion on topics ranging from current events to calendaring. We have discussed the week's *parashah* at a deep level, relevant dilemmas in our greater community, marking transitions in the life of a Millennial, the role of social justice for overcommitted professionals, how to build and sustain boards and lay leaders, Tishah B'Av for modern Jews, employing the best methods for social media, and more. The host is responsible for setting an agenda, focusing the group on a clear theme for the day's discussion. All topics are valuable and all discussions fruitful. Sometimes we ruminate at the thirty-thousand-foot level. Sometimes we dig into the nitty-gritty details. Sometimes we just need a safe space to talk through frustrations and challenges.

We meet over lunch, intentionally carving out time in our workday. In a two-hour meeting, much of our time is dedicated to schmoozing, reflecting, and simply being together. Indeed, a community is not built by how many points are on the agenda but instead through relationships formed by everyone who sits at the table. Our relationships with colleagues are possibly the most meaningful rewards of our Engager Network.

Challenges and Opportunities: The Art of *Tzimtzum*

The philosophy for the approach and framework of our Engager Network is based on a powerful Jewish concept, one far older than our group or the Millennials we serve. Isaac Luria and the Kabbalists speak of *tzimtzum*, God's act of contracting from the universe in order to inspire Creation itself. God performed this act willingly, teaching the crucial principle of humility and the need to pull oneself back to let others emerge, thereby unleashing their power and potential.

Dr. Eugene Borowitz, in his preeminent 1974 article, "*Tzimtzum:* A Mystic Model for Contemporary Leadership,"[8] teaches God's act of *tzimtzum* to be one of "inculcating compassion in the possessors of power, that is, all of us . . . Rather than rely on a sovereign's goodwill we prefer to share [God's] power. So today almost every social arrangement we know is under pressure to transform itself in the direction of a more effective democracy."

These words have been intentionally or inadvertently embraced by the Millennial generation, a group to which both of us belong. Our collective social arrangement is firmly built on a collaborative model, one where additional points of view can be helpful and working together is far more effective than working apart; where we acknowledge times to speak up and, equally as important, times to listen.

Borowitz's words ring true forty years later in the libraries, conference rooms, and meeting spaces of Jewish organizations of greater Seattle. The goal of our Engager Network is the creation of a greater community. We share our power, our knowledge, and our excitement. The larger, better-resourced organizations do not dictate and the smaller ones do not acquiesce. Everyone has a voice at the table and everyone makes an important contribution.

Tzimtzum is an art. It takes patience and requires trust in those around you. It is also a constantly evolving endeavor. Our Network shifts as professionals come and go. Our levels of participation within the Network shift as the demands of our full-time jobs ebb and flow. Participating in the work of *tzimtzum* means not only knowing when to step forward and when to encourage others to do so; it means being communicative and transparent with your colleagues. Only then can we move forward and grow.

There is the old trope that Jewish organizations can be deeply territorial; so concerned about numbers that they keep their best ideas close to the chest. This perpetuates the myth that Jewish engagement is a zero-sum game. While each of us certainly wants our organization to succeed, we know that one group's success does not forecast the fall of another. In fact, the opposite is true. As the old maxim goes, "A rising tide lifts all boats." Through our work with the Engager Network, each of our groups has grown, whether through attendance, increased funding, the nurturing of new programs, delivering richer content, or simply being recognized as "stronger, better, and more meaningful" by our participants.

The message we share with the greater young adult community is this: We as an Engager Network do not compete with one another; we work together so that everyone can succeed. We work hard so that all Seattle's Jewish young adults can access multiple opportunities to connect to Jewish life. We commit to this so individuals can nurture a Jewish identity, create a Jewish home, seek Jewish outlets for themselves and their family, and participate in the meaningful journey of expanding an ever-evolving Jewish soul. We work hard, practicing the art of *tzimtzum* and sharing the space of young adult engagement because it's the right thing to do.

As Borowitz's article implies, we contract ourselves to let others in. In this way, we end up creating far more and being infinitely more successful at engaging those whom we all collectively serve.

In Closing

Why is the Seattle Engager Network a success? There is no magic formula or rubric. We follow a similar pattern and adjust or change as the need arises. We pick a date. The host picks the topic. And together we meet: all equals, regardless of years of experience, and all partners, regardless of our organization's size or success. We learn, create, and lead together. As a result of our shared efforts, we have seen a rise in participation and enthusiasm in our programs and organizations. Our promotional material is vastly stronger, as we are advertising for one another and reaching a larger number of Millennials around the city. And more than the numbers and the data, our success is defined by a proud feeling that our organizations support one another and support the larger goal of Millennial engagement. Frequently, those who attend our events comment on the refreshing attitude of inclusion, shared future, and cooperation that our Engager Network creates. This value supersedes all statistics in the world and yields so much more.

When we leave our Engager Network meetings we feel excited to try something new and continue collaborating with and learning from each other. We feel less alone in our work as Jewish professionals. The Engager Network is not just another meeting on our calendar. It is a sacred space of trust, respect, and sharing—a space to talk through each other's quandaries and celebrate each other's victories.

We believe our Network is a model adaptable for any city. We have no budget, though each one of us will often cover the cost of lunch or snacks for our peers to share. We have no one central leader or organizer. While Jconnect may have been the initial convener, the largest organization no longer needs to take the lead. We have our philosophy of collaboration and we have one another. That's our recipe for success and it's worked for us.

As for adapting this model to other cities, we encourage each of you to start small but think big: Create and sustain a network of professionals from across the spectrum of organizations that exist in your area. Perhaps begin with a *b'rit*, laying out principles that suggest openness and support. We urge you to hold meetings regularly without fail, always with a flexible agenda. Keep an open seat for anyone willing to participate, and most importantly, move one another toward a broader shared goal for your work, both individual and collective. Remember that those who sit across the table from you are your greatest allies of all.

Just as we create and continue to create what is right for us, so too we hope you can create what is right for you. Who knows where our Engager Network will be in another year and a half? For now, we look forward to the next time we will all get together and work to build a place for Seattle Jewish Millennials to call home.

Notes

1. The 2014 Greater Seattle Jewish Community Study, sponsored by the Jewish Federation of Greater Seattle, research conducted by Matthew Boxer, Janet Krasner, Matthew A. Brown, and Leonard Saxe, Cohen Center for Modern Jewish Studies, Steinhardt Research Institute, Brandeis University (2014), https://www.jewishinseattle.org/sites/default/files/Community_Study_FINAL.pdf.
2. Joanna Piacenza and Robert P. Jones, "The Top Two Religious Groups That Dominate American Cities," Public Religion Research Institute (August 3, 2015), http://www.prri.org/spotlight/the-top-two-religious-traditions-that-dominate-american-cities/#.Vb-2Z-1Viko%20--.
3. "2013 Pew Research Center: A Portrait of Jewish Americans," Pew Research Center (October 1, 2013), http://www.pewforum.org/2013/10/01/jewish-american-beliefs-attitudes-culture-survey/.
4. Birthright Next has since ceased operations on June 30, 2015.
5. Dan Fast and Adam Pollack, "A 5-Point Plan to Build Your Local Engager Network," Jim Joseph Foundation (May 26, 2015), https://jimjosephfoundation.org/a-5-point-plan-to-build-your-local-engager-network/.
6. Jconnect Seattle (http://www.jconnectseattle.org) is a program of Hillel UW and has the mission of "[creating] a meaningful Jewish

life for 21–35 year olds through diverse communities and innovative experiences."
7. These questions are attributed to Elise Peizner and Josh Furman, who distributed them at the original Engager meeting.
8. Eugene Borowitz, "Tzimtzum: A Mystic Model for Contemporary Leadership," *Religious Education* 69, no. 6 (November–December 1974):687–700.

Investing in Our Infrastructure: Why Congregations Matter Now More Than Ever

Aaron Miller

A Roman matron once asked Rabbi Yosi what God has been doing since the six days of creation. Rabbi Yosi replied, "The Holy Blessed One sits and matches couples; the daughter of this one to this one, the wife of this one, to this one . . ." The matron replied to Rabbi Yosi, "And this is God's occupation? Even I could do so! How many male and female servants I have! In a moment I could match them." Rabbi Yosi replied, "If it is easy in your eyes, it is as difficult in the eyes of the Holy Blessed One as splitting the Red Sea"[1]

In the congregational work that many rabbis do, there is no one metric to evaluate our success or failure. Do congregants like our sermons? Are we able to support families who have lost loved ones? Do we offer comfort in the hospital? Do our *b'nei mitzvah* students feel at home when reading Torah? Do adult learners enjoy our classes? Do we collaborate well with lay leadership? When evaluating a congregational rabbi, the metrics are fuzzy.

Expectations seem more straightforward when evaluating outreach to Jewish Millenials. In addition to the usual responsibilities of a congregational rabbi, I run 2239,[2] Washington Hebrew Congregation's young professional community for DC-area Reform Jews between the ages of 22 and 39. With the invaluable support of my senior rabbi, Bruce Lustig, my clergy colleagues, the Washington Hebrew staff, our congregational leaders, and a visionary team of young professionals, Washington Hebrew's 2239 has grown exponentially over the years. Our monthly Shabbat experience, Metro Minyan, gathers in large venues near one of DC's metro stations,

---

AARON MILLER (C11) is Associate Rabbi of Washington Hebrew Congregation in Washington, DC, and Director of 2239, the Congregation's outreach to young professionals.

drawing in 150 to 250 (or more) young Jewish professionals to celebrate Shabbat together. We inspire commitment to *tikkun olam* through service-learning opportunities in DC and throughout the nation. We read Jewish books together, and our Passover seders and High Holy Day services are always at capacity. Yet with the Millennial outreach work I do, the metrics seem to boil down to one: how many Jews have met and gotten married?

As a rabbi serving Jewish Millennials, I am asked this question subtly or more overtly whenever I describe my work. So when it comes up, I put on a smile and talk about Brian and Michelle. Brian, by his admission, had not been Jewishly engaged since graduating college. He then went on a 2239 service-learning trip to New Orleans and reconnected to Judaism more deeply than ever before. Brian started attending Metro Minyan, where a few months later, he met a Jewish woman named Michelle. After dating for a year and a half, Brian proposed to Michelle at Metro Minyan in the same room where they first met.

I love this story. I love losing count of how many Millennial Jews, both gay and straight, come to 2239 events, meet each other, and leave together (I assume to study that week's *parashah*, or whatever else Millennials might do together on a Friday night). Jews absolutely meet each other at 2239 events, and my rabbinate is full of anecdotes.

But underneath it all, I am filled with anxiety and can understand Rabbi Yosi's hesitation. Getting people to fall in love is God's work, not some project for a Roman matron—or even a rabbi. I am anxious because I know that numbers are more honest than any anecdote I may collect over the years. Looking out in the pews of 200 Jewish Millennials who may come to a Metro Minyan any given month, statistics suggest that 142 of them, 71 percent of America's non-Orthodox Jewish Millennials, will marry non-Jews. And that's just the intermarriage rate reported by the 2013 Pew study. Writing now three years later, that number is likely higher and will continue to rise.

1,325,000. This is roughly the number of Jewish Millennials in the United States, and this is the number that keeps me up at night.[3] To be clear, "Jewish" is as hard to define as it is to count the number of Millennials who fit that description, but with Millennials making up a quarter of the U.S. adult Jewish population of 5.3 million, any solution that is not scalable to 1.3 million is not going to do what we need it to do. If in-marriage is our primary goal when engaging the next generation of Jews, we have just said goodbye to 71 percent of our future. About 1 million Jews have just been shown the door, and they probably will not miss us very much.

"How many Jews are meeting each other, marrying, and having children?" This is only one facet of an increasingly complex question. Decades ago, this was the most important question we, Jewish professionals and philanthropists, could ask, because in-marriage seemed to be the only thing that could inoculate the Jewish future against assimilation. But the twenty-first century has exposed the uncomfortable truth. The greatest challenge facing progressive Judaism is not Jews marrying Christians or Muslims or atheists, but Jews who have left their Judaism behind. If we don't make Judaism matter to the largest generation in American history, nothing else is going to work.

If the purpose of Millennial Jewish programming is to get Jews to meet each other and have Jewish babies, then online dating might have been our silver bullet. But are transformative Jewish experiences—Shabbat, *tikkun olam*, adult-level learning—simply less effective attempts to do what JDate or JSwipe or JWed do already? The end goal of Millennial Judaism needs to be more than marriage. In order to reach it, we need to ask a better question: *How can we, the Reform Movement, get Judaism to matter more?* What if our goal was not, "How can we get more Jews to fall in love with Jews?" but instead, "How can we get more Jews to fall in love with being Jewish?" What if, regardless of who our Millennials date and marry, they have been so inspired by Jewish living that the families they create together will be Jewish?

Given the daunting challenges of 21st century Jewish demographics listed elsewhere in this journal, fighting apathy is a more worthy battle than combatting intermarriage—and one we actually can win. Study after study shows that many modern Jews care less about being Jewish than any previous generation. Blame anything you want—religious school or *b'nei mitzvah* preparation or membership dues—but the whole picture is much more interesting. For a generation coming of age in a world of increasingly bewildering complexity, pediatric religious tradition does not stand a chance. The only Millennial initiatives that will work in the long run are those that inspire a deep connection to adult Judaism. Millennial life will always feel busy, harried, and overwhelming, but adult Judaism is what can keep us grounded and connected. Adult Judaism—the kind that inspires and challenges the soul—is what makes adult life meaningful, and Millennials are hungry for meaning.

Where can today's Jews find meaning? There are dozens of new projects around Millennial engagement—emerging Jewish communities designed and funded to uniquely serve the needs of young, progressive Jewish adults. They are led by inspiring, charismatic (and often young) rabbis who lead rousing worship experiences on Friday nights and major holidays and get Millennial turnout that most brick-and-mortar congregations can only dream of. But then what? Assume that two Jewish Millennials meet, fall in love with each other, and through their inspiring Jewish communities, fall in love with Judaism at the same time. They get married, have children, buy that minivan and a Costco membership . . . then what? What happens when they, our demographic success stories, inevitably age and/or have a life-cycle event that takes them out of the Millennial community they once called home? What about their kids who need nursery school or parents who seek daytime programming as retirees? What about future bar and bat mitzvahs, trips to Israel, and enduring communal relationships? These emerging initiatives are not only prohibitively expensive for most communities around the country, but they fall short in providing Millennials with a lifelong Jewish home.

Based on my experience with Washington Hebrew's 2239, I would like to suggest an imperfect solution: congregations. Not congregations without walls. Not congregations that meet online. Brick-and-mortar congregations, with rabbis and cantors and copy machines—the very kind that we have been trying to work around for all these years. What if congregations assumed the lion's share for engaging the next generation and filling the yawning gap between college graduation and nursery school enrollment?

Most Jewish Millennials do not feel at home in today's congregations. We can blame membership policies or worship styles or the dozen other things that Jewish leaders and philanthropists fairly (or unfairly) criticize. But congregations are the key to the Jewish future because in scope and scale, nothing else in our tradition has the potential to address the needs of 1.3 million Jewish Millennials. In our people's brightest and darkest moments, the Jewish need to congregate, organize, connect to God, and connect to each other, has remained stubbornly fixed. Congregations are and have always been the infrastructure of the Jewish people, and an investment in our Jewish infrastructure will pay dividends for generations to come.

In the penultimate episode of the political drama *West Wing*, C. J. Cregg, one of the series' main characters, is considering her next career after serving as the White House Chief of Staff. After a number of flashy proposals, she finally meets with Franklin Hollis, a nanotech billionaire, who describes a charity he is starting that he would like C. J. to lead:

> Hollis: I want to find a single problem I can attack. Something which might actually have some kind of substantial effect. Maybe I should be fighting AIDS in Africa. Or maybe it's malaria. Could be clean air or election reform. I don't know. But my sense is that you would have a unique perspective on what that could be and how to make it happen.
>
> C. J.: A single problem.
>
> Hollis: It's a complicated question . . .
>
> C. J. (interrupting): Highways—Is what you're looking for.
>
> Hollis: Really?
>
> C. J.: It's not sexy. No one will ever raise money for it. But nine out of ten African aid projects fail because the medicine or the personnel can't get to the people in need. Infrastructure's a problem . . . Blanket the continent with highways and then maybe get started on plumbing.
>
> Hollis: Also not sexy.
>
> C. J.: Makes for a lousy telethon.
>
> Hollis: Well, if you think that's what needs fixing, I'll give you $10 billion to fix it.

Congregations are the infrastructure of the Jewish people. In the Reform Movement alone, there are over 850 communities ranging from small student pulpits to 2,000-plus family, multi-campus institutions. Congregations might not sound flashy, but if anything can touch the lives of even a fraction of our country's 1.3 million Jewish Millennials, it is our movement's congregations. In sheer numbers alone, no other model comes close.

This does not always mean that congregations work for Millennials, and again, it largely comes down to the numbers. High-quality

Millennial programming is expensive, and with shrinking memberships, congregational budgets are already stretched. If a synagogue board of trustees has to choose between rising insurance premiums or a new Shabbat experience for nonmember 20- and 30-somethings, the financial concern of the day will usually win. This is why Millennial Jewish programming, where it exists, often takes the form of baseball games, happy hours, and kickball teams. These events are relatively easy to plan, they typically break even, and there's a good chance people will show up. But they fail to inspire and challenge the Jewish soul.

What if we could mitigate congregations' very real financial concerns with modest and sustainable investments in the congregations themselves? What if congregations received philanthropic support to do the important outreach they are longing to do, not just in Washington or Los Angeles or New York, but in cities throughout the country where Millennial Jews have few if any options to connect? Washington Hebrew Congregation's 2239 model works in Washington, DC, but imagine if established congregations in other cities could apply for seed money to address the specific needs of the Millennials in their communities. What if there were a national fund that Reform Movement–affiliated congregations could access to offset the initial startup costs? What if there were training initiatives for clergy who are passionate about next-gen work and publications for congregations and their rabbis to collaborate on together? What if we made it a little easier for congregations to do the groundbreaking work our 1.3 million Millennials need them to do? What if the Reform Movement turned outreach and engagement of Jewish college graduates and young professionals into its own kind of movement?

Imagine if our leading Jewish philanthropists came together—as they have for our movement's camps, Hillel, or Birthright Israel—to invest in congregational infrastructure. Imagine if even a fraction of our movement's hundreds of congregations now had the financial capacity to launch Millennial Shabbat experiences, Torah study groups, or *tikkun olam* initiatives. These transformative Jewish experiences often require clergy; what if this funding reimbursed the congregation for part of its clergy's efforts in order to defray the costs of their time? In funding preexisting congregations, these precious philanthropic dollars wouldn't need to go towards copy machines or insurance premiums—the congregation is already paying for those. They would go directly toward the highest quality programming a congregation can provide for a generation that needs it most.

While it might not be flashy, philanthropic support of our movement's congregations is efficient and sustainable, leveraging existing resources to transform Millennial engagement one city at a time. I am proud of the work Washington Hebrew has done in our city, but when it comes down to numbers, does it matter if our monthly Metro Minyan attendance is 200 or 400? When it comes to the 1.3 million Jewish Millennials across the country, the success of our one initiative ultimately changes very little. The right funding model, however, can transform our nation's congregations into the driving force behind next-generation engagement on a scale that can change the tide. When we invest in our Jewish infrastructure, the other seemingly intractable problems facing twenty-first-century Jewry will start to fall into place.

Talk to any temple president or membership director, and congregations are desperate for Millennials. You need not be a demographer to know that the day will soon come when most new members of our congregations will be Millennials. If we want them, we need to get ready for them now.

Millennials need congregations as much as congregations need Millennials. Millennials are searching for connection, spirituality, and meaning. They crave learning, passion, and to join a community of people devoted to improving our world. At its best, this is what congregational life can be. Millennials do not need another dating service, and rabbis cannot make people fall in love. But congregations are where our people forever connect to the sacred in our world and the sacred in one another.

We are the infrastructure of the Jewish people.

Notes

1. *B'reisheet Rabba* 68:4
2. The name refers to the age range of the constituency—22 through 39 years-old.
3. Pew Research Center Survey of U.S. Jews, conducted February 20 to June 13, 2013.

Mind of a Millennial

Millennial Engagement and the Problem of Loneliness

Marc Katz

Today, our communities use many verbs to describe our relationship to Millennials. Inside the walls of synagogues and other Jewish institutions it is common to hear words like "engage" or "involve." We provide them with free programs and allocate rabbinic time to them through grants and congregational subsidies. Our leading philanthropists fly them to Israel with the hope that upon their return they connect with organized Jewish life. While all of these actions are important, they miss a fundamental truth about the experience of many Millennials; many are incredibly lonely.

Whether struggling with the isolation of moving to a new city or living at home, whether endeavoring to find a job or keep a new one, whether looking for a life partner or dealing with an unhappy relationship, loneliness can touch almost any part of their lives. However, if our institutions fail to use the primary verbs of our human experiences—to see, to comfort, to nurture, to connect—we will have missed the opportunity to meet Millennials at their most profound and important moments. Ironically, we will fail to "engage" or "involve" the rising generation of Millennials until we meet their underlying human needs. Responding to the loneliness that defines the existence of all Millennials is key to bringing them to (or bringing them back to) Jewish community.

In his book, *The Lonely Man of Faith,* Rabbi Joseph Soloveitchik explains that each of us is made of a "majestic" personality and

---

RABBI MARC KATZ (NY12) is the associate rabbi at Congregation Beth Elohim. He is the author of the recent book *The Heart of Loneliness: How Jewish Wisdom Can Help You Cope and Find Comfort* (Jewish Lights).

a "covenantal" personality. The former seeks fulfillment through achievement. It is the engine of scientific achievement and the agar dish of power. It is the high that we get when we work a room, the rush after a successful presentation, the pride that makes us reach higher, stand taller, and work harder. It is the part of us that wants to conquer, to own, to dominate.

Our covenantal personality, however, is not interested in those things. It wants connection and love. It wants openness and honesty, presence and purpose. It cares less of winning than being. Popularity is irrelevant. It would rather be seen by a few then be known by many. When we neglect our covenantal selves, loneliness and alienation follows.

As rabbis, it's much easier to address the majestic aspects of our Jewish community. We seek to put on large events, hoping that if we fill a room with enough people we might foster friendships while knowing full well that often the loneliest experience of all can be felt in crowds we do not know. We bring in interesting speakers who engage the mind but fail to move the heart. We encourage others at services to connect with God but fail to foster human connection. We gather to make sandwiches for the nameless, give care to the faceless, collect money for the disaster while ignoring the person. We too often count heads rather than souls.

Loneliness is addressed through deliberate attention to the covenantal selves of others and while there is no magic bullet, our institutions can play an important role in addressing this often-precarious part of our personalities.

Making Others Feel They Matter

Anyone who steps through our door must get the message that they matter to us. Our tradition likens each person to a cistern, with deep crevices and secret passageways (*B'reishit Rabbah* 24:1). The more of these that remain hidden, the less we feel seen. There is a reason that the traditional blessing when we see a group of people is "Blessed are you God ... the knower of secrets" (*B'rachot* 58a). We are an enigma. Loneliness often follows when we feel that what others know about us does not resemble what we know about ourselves. We, as a community, should send a message to all of those who enter our buildings that they can unlock the box that contains their true selves and that we will meet them with openness and love. When they do, we can then give honor to our collective woundedness and become the salve that allows all them, and us, to heal.

Looking for Our Stories in Those of Our Ancestors

It often feels that we are the only one dealing with our struggles. We think that no one has experienced a divorce or loss like ours. No one can understand my struggles with dating, the challenges of my marriage, the isolation of living alone. However, others have walked the path before us—and in treading upon the same rocky ground, have taught us where we might step and where we might falter. In the Bible, Abraham, Isaac, and Joseph all faced loss in their lives. In the Talmud, Honi and Rabbi Yochanan struggled with the alienation of finding lasting and meaningful friendships. Midrash is filled with stories like Eve and Miriam's bad marriages. Hagar can become a model of the pain of divorce.

The scope of Judaism, however, is vast. There is a reason our ancient Rabbis likened its texts and teachings to a sea. A lifetime is barely enough to scratch the surface. Our leaders and institutions must act as guides in helping people to find these stories. Whether they bring insight; whether they promote comfort; whether they enrich, nurture, or strengthen us is helpful but beside the point. More than anything, the presence of these stories can tell us that although our loneliness may feel like a barren island, it is not. Others have walked there before us; in seeing this, we are no longer alone.

Helping Others Find Purpose

Friedrich Nietzsche once wrote, "He who has a Why to live for can bear almost any How."[1] Judaism can aid in fostering meaning. When we see a role for ourselves in this world, it becomes a much less lonely place. Whether it is the mandate to make the world better, the quest to seek spiritual connection, or the will to bring beauty into this world, knowing that you have a unique purpose fosters passion and brings weight to your actions. How often do we greet someone at an event by telling them about the next one? Wouldn't it be more powerful to hear from them where their passions lay? When we engage deeply with something we love, others take note. In the moment of purpose we bear our spirit and in our ardour let others in. It's no wonder that some of my deepest friendships have formed in the midst of my most engaging pastimes.

Fostering Moments of Solitude

Too many of us rely on our phones to stay connected. We are so joined to others in a superficial and instant way that we have lost the ability to be alone. Solitude doesn't always lead to loneliness. We have all had wonderful experiences without the company of others. Rabbi Nachman used to meditate alone in the forest in a process he called *hitbodedut*. Henry David Thoreau once called solitude his "greatest companion." Today, how many of us can say this? Many fear solitude, choosing to ignore the self through distraction rather than engage with it. Loneliness follows when we are forced to face a solitude for which we are not ready or open. Judaism, through introspection, prayer, meditation, and study can foster a greater understanding of the self. For brief periods, Jewish communities, especially on Shabbat, can ask others to put away their phones, providing the space for self reflection and self love that we can take with us when we leave and find ourselves alone.

Creating Moments of Triumph

Though crowds and community are not synonymous, it is possible for large groups of people to achieve cohesion. We have all been together at concerts or rallies and felt as if we were a part of something bigger than ourselves. Our shared purpose or spiritual experience becomes an organism unto itself, alive and real. While personal relationships are the foundation of any approach to dealing with loneliness, moments of communal transcendence can turn the alienation of the group into something comforting and profound. We should strive, through singing, prayer, and study to break down the walls that exist between us and to connect on a deeper spiritual plane. The goal at any communal gathering is to yearn together, to join hands and seek something greater. We as leaders can model our yearnings and our searchings and can foster the bravery in our congregants to do the same. Then when we least expect it, the alienation of the crowd will morph into the power of community.

Conclusion

The problem with much of our twenties/thirties programming is that it does none of these. Catchy names and advertising gets people in the door, but once they arrive do we do enough to assure that everyone leaves feeling seen? What's funny is that to help those who are lonely, we don't need to be more creative (feeding our majestic impulse). We need to be more deliberate (nurturing our covenantal selves). The same class can be alienating and intimidating, with people showing off how much they know and ancient wisdom appearing no more relevant than trivia. Or, it can provide a platform for self and communal exploration, providing moments for us to connect to our neighbors, driving us toward purpose and meaning. The same service can feel foreign and mechanical (even as we dress it up with a band and cocktails). Or, it can create a communal spirit that makes us know we belong and can give us the strength to introduce ourselves to someone new.

Our Jewish communities cannot solve all instances of loneliness in our communities. We can't make a loss hurt less. We can't make someone fall in love. We can't repair a broken relationship. One who is lonely must learn to have the trust and strength to reach out and to seek comfort in the arms of others. But we can do something just as profound. We can create an ethos where when someone is ready, they know they have a platform to be seen, where they can enter into a community that cares and they can find kindred spirits in the people of today and the texts of old.

We often wonder why Millennials come and go, fleeting in and out of our communities and programs. In truth, Judaism is not the most important thing in their lives. To say so belittles the power of lived experience. Judaism, as an idea, will never be more important than the loss of a parent or the inability to find a job. Faced with loneliness from any number of sources, if Judaism and the Jewish community doesn't have anything to offer us when we are suffering in those moments, then it loses its relevance. Though our programming may be top notch, healing from a death or dealing with isolation are much more pressing. If our community does not address these, if Judaism has nothing to say when we are feeling the most lonely and in need of comfort, then what's the point of all this?

Note

1. I first encountered this quote in Harold Kushner's forward to Viktor Frankl, Man's Search For *Meaning* (Boston: Beacon Press, 2006).

Jewish Millennials and Millennial Judaism

Kerry M. Olitzky

In September 2016, the Steinhardt Social Research Institute's American Jewish Population Project published data that 1.4 million Jewish Millennials currently live in the United States and comprise one quarter of Jewish adults.[1] As we bear witness to the rapid rise of this generation, institutional Judaism grapples with the declining affiliation rates of Jewish Millennials.[2] We need to better understand what Judaism means to them, what the role of Judaism can be or should be in their lives, and what our institutions can do as they have with every successive generation: adapt to help Millennials thrive through Jewish experience, wisdom, and community.

Big Tent Judaism initiated a study in Summer 2016 to learn more about the experience of being Jewish among Jewish Millennials and to better understand how this population demonstrates its connection to being Jewish. Because this population appears to be elusive and hard to reach, all inquiry into this population is important. The study defined experiences broadly to include anything that a Jewish Millennial does that makes her/him feel Jewish, including experiences beyond the "traditional" ways of being Jewish such as going to synagogue, keeping kosher, or celebrating holidays.

The study included a combination of quantitative and qualitative data collection and analysis. The quantitative portion of the study included a set of multiple-choice and scaled-item questions in an online survey of nearly six hundred. The study

---

KERRY M. OLITZKY, DHL (C81) is the executive director of Big Tent Judaism, a national, independent, transdenominational organization reaching out to unaffiliated Jewish families with an emphasis on engaging those who have intermarried. Formerly, he served as vice president of the Wexner Heritage Foundation and national dean of Adult Jewish Learning and Living of HUC-JIR.

included a series of open-ended survey questions conducted primarily as an optional section of the quantitative survey as well as one-on-one interviews conducted by staff members of Big Tent Judaism.

Additionally, we conducted seventy-five in-depth interviews in person, as well as on the telephone. In many cases, the respondents were the same as those who participated in the online survey and volunteered to participate in a follow-up interview. While the limited sample size of these in-depth interviews makes it difficult to determine trends, they helped offer additional illustration and color to the survey data.[3]

Quantitative Data

The results of this study help build on existing knowledge regarding Jewish Millennials' participation in activities, rituals, and organizations, as well as perceptions of their Jewish identity. Eighty percent of the respondents in this survey reported that they do Jewish things either a moderate amount, quite a bit, or very much. They are engaged in Jewish activities, rituals, and organizations to varying degrees, and although they indicate that participating in rituals makes them feel the most Jewish, they are more engaged in social aspects of Jewish life (e.g., Jewish friends and food). Overall, less than half of the respondents believe in God, but almost all respondents (at least in some ways) think that their personal values are related to their being Jewish.

The results support the notion that, in addition to the traditional ways in which people have engaged in Jewish ritual, there are many opportunities for further connections to Jewish identity through social and cultural avenues. Specific results that support this notion include:

- Approximately 40 percent of respondents indicate that someone has said or done something that made them question their Jewish identity. This suggests that Millennials need more and varied opportunities to feel a part of and connected to Judaism.
- To a great extent, respondents report that, overall, participating in Jewish activities and organizations make them feel Jewish, at least some of the time. So, while traditional rituals are important to them too in terms of a strong connection to

Jewish identity, activities and organizations present important avenues for feeling Jewish as well.
- Time is a barrier for all respondents, which highlights the need to provide Millennials with opportunities to participate Jewishly in ways that fit their schedules and consistent with how Millennials are used to living their lives (e.g., online and when and where they want). For the 20 percent of respondents who indicated that they do Jewish things not at all or a little bit, other barriers also become salient and important to pay attention to, such as lack of interest in participating, having friends who are not Jewish, not having good experiences in the past, relevancy of participation, and having negative experiences in Jewish social settings. The implication for these barriers is that Millennials' engagement in Jewish life needs to be supported in ways that make people feel most comfortable and included. This notion and many detailed explanations regarding how to best include Millennials are addressed in the greater-detail qualitative portions of this study which follow.
- The prevailing identity for respondents is that they are "Jewish" and to a lesser extent associating with an identity that is affiliated with organized synagogue life. This, plus the results related to belief in God, suggest that these categories can be challenging places for Millennials to feel comfortable.

The results of the quantitative portion of the study, as well as the supporting themes from the qualitative components, point to an important way in which Millennials need to be engaged in Jewish life. Specifically, a focus on a cultural approach to Judaism is needed, one that promotes inclusiveness, flexibility of participation, and multiple ways in which engagement is seen as acceptable (i.e., through activities, rituals, and organizations). For example, productive experiences around Shabbat that promote engagement, include participating in nonthreatening rituals as well as social opportunities, such as enjoying food together. Helping Millennials socialize and experience Judaism in a manner consistent with the way the generation interacts with one another can promote stronger engagement and desire to participate in Jewish life. It is important that these needs are responded to in order to foster strong connections for this generation to the Jewish community.

Qualitative Trends

Respondents to the open-ended survey questions and participants in the in-depth interviews offered additional language and illustration that articulated information beyond the bounds of our quantitative study. Like the quantitative data we compiled, since this is a report reflecting those who opted in (i.e., people who chose to participate in the research project), it is difficult to draw a set of universal conclusions about engaging this generation. Nonetheless, there are many lessons that we learned, many of which affirm what we already know about Millennials, in general, and Jewish Millennials, in particular. However, these insights do extend our knowledge beyond the previous boundaries, including those made public in recent reports. They also allow us to make suggestions to Jewish communal professionals and Jewish communal volunteer leaders as to how to engage the Millennial population, as well as the benefits of doing so.

- Whether they are more engaged by the community than their peers or more distant from it, the complaints about the Jewish community from those who are engaged are often the same as criticisms from those who are not engaged in the community. This is also true of their suggestions for how to engage more people among the Millennial generation.
- Even among those who are actively involved, and those who are proud to be Jewish, they have experienced times in which the Jewish community has been unwelcoming to them. These experiences make them more cautious about further engagement with the organized community and its institutions.
- The Millennials who participated in our research project often described themselves as grappling with contemporary Israel and with American social justice issues. This is an important reflection of the time period in which they were born.
- Even for those who are Jewishly active, they may not describe themselves as being spiritual or see Judaism as fulfilling their spiritual needs.
- Beyond time and cost, there were two items mentioned by almost all of the respondents: the synagogue and the organized Jewish community are not adapting to meet the expressed needs of the generation. This is a particular challenge as the

generation finds itself in the historical trajectory several generations away from the immigrant experience of American Jews.
- Those things that they identify as being Jewish represent a wide panoply of activities and are generally not confined to taking place in one institution. Even those who are active Jewishly have episodic connections with numerous institutions. This is even the case among those who are dues-paying members of an institution.
- The respondents tend to consider themselves more actively Jewish than might otherwise seem obvious by their responses. Thus, measurements for engagement must be expanded, especially beyond the organized Jewish community.
- While respondents tend to mark Jewish time (holidays and the like), they are more likely to do so outside of the institutions that are part of the landscape of the organized Jewish community. This is a trend that we see in other population segments, as well, but it seems more pronounced among Millennials. There may be some leakage from one generation to another.
- Like other generations at this point in American Jewish history, this generation has difficulty trying to define the notion of Jewish community—as well as its relation to it.
- Family-of-origin (that is, their Jewish upbringing) and their Jewish education contributed to how they now feel about being Jewish. But they couldn't really identify what is essential to being Jewish or acting Jewish.
- An inclusive Jewish community (the welcoming of a variety of subgroups including those who are LGBTQ and those who have intermarried) is an important condition for participation for many respondents.

Program Recommendations

1. Since Millennials have limited discretionary time, help them to understand the benefit of participating in the community or in a program. (Make sure you understand the benefit first and can articulate it.) This will allow them to spend their expressed limited commodity of time more wisely. A subset of this issue: cost may be a factor, but the cost benefit is even more important and must also be shared with them.

2. Provide them with opportunities for leadership. Don't make them earn it over time. If you choose to wait, they will find these opportunities elsewhere or build their own institutions (e.g., start-ups, independent minyanim, and the "emergent communities"). And make sure that authority accompanies responsibility.
3. Stop privileging members over those who want an episodic connection with an institution or program or a group of institutions or programs. This will help increase their feeling of belonging.
4. Offer alternative membership models for those who seek it, recognizing that many will not want it. But without such alternatives, you will not be able to reach them at all.
5. Discontinue social mixers as a primary programming model. Single Millennials are looking for more from the Jewish community than social mixers, but they may be looking for social events. Similarly, there is a gap in programming for Millennial couples who do not have children. Of special note: there is an increasing number of single mothers by choice who may require special program attention.
6. Provide a context—and safe space—for civil discourse regarding Israel.
7. Partner with other community organizations (outside of the Jewish community), especially those with a social justice agenda.
8. Provide them with opportunities to actually experience the Divine rather than just talk about it or assume that traditional vehicles accomplish the task. For that segment of the population who are humanists and do not believe in God, affirm that belief as legitimate and authentic (since Judaism has always been more interested in what people do rather than in what they believe).
9. Like other population segments, Millennials are more likely to access Judaism at holiday time. While some may be in close geographic proximity to their parents, and others will return "home" for the holidays, many will celebrate with their local friends rather than travel to be with their family. Thus, use the holidays as a primary vehicle to reach them—in informal contexts with their friends. Encourage them to get together with friends and provide them with program

support and resources to do so. But don't push them into traditional modes of observance and participation.
10. Be transparent. This generation abhors the lack of transparency prevalent in some Jewish institutions.

While there is no guarantee that the application of these strategies will bring more Millennials into engagement with Judaism and the Jewish community, it is quite certain that without the implementation of these strategies, we run the risk of losing a large segment of this population, perhaps an entire generation. There are many forces in the world that are pulling at them. And if we push them away from the Jewish community through inaction, or with an unwillingness to change and adapt to meet their expressed needs and observed behaviors, then the various forces pulling at them will be made even stronger. And we will be diminished as a community as a result.

Notes

1. http://ajpp.brandeis.edu/infosheets/Millennials.php.
2. http://www.pewforum.org/2013/10/01/jewish-american-beliefs-attitudes-culture-survey/.
3. The complete report may be found here: http://bigtentjudaism.org/uploads/MILLENNIAL-ENGAGEMENT-IN-THE-JEWISH-COMMUNITY-2016-Full-Report.pdf.

Breast Practices: How a Lactation Support Group Taught Me the Possibility of Jewish Community

Amanda Schwartz

In many ways, I defy what statistics say about Millennials. Though I fall within the generation, I'm pretty much as affiliated with Judaism as possible: I'm not only a member of a synagogue but I'm a rabbi! And yet despite looking like a poster child for being a Jewishly affiliated Millennial, I too have experienced the same lack of meaning and community in traditional Jewish settings and have sought it outside of the Jewish institutions that I know and love. In the study "How We Gather" Angie Thurston and Casper ter Kuile write, "As traditional religion struggles to attract young people, Millennials are looking elsewhere with increasing urgency. And in some cases, they are creating what they don't find."[1] This is my story of failing in the Jewish community, looking for meaning elsewhere, and creating what I didn't find.

What Does Millennial Community Look Like?

During rabbinical school, I served as a rabbinic intern at a synagogue that received a grant to serve the twenties/thirties demographic. At the end of the year, I felt like a failure. The grant report asked me all about the number of participants per event and in particular new participants. Though we had a few large events with 50 to 150 people, most of our programs were monthly Shabbat dinners with about 10 to 15 people. And many of these people were the same people month after month. The synagogue I worked for hoped that the twenties/thirties participants would not only come

---

RABBI AMANDA SCHWARTZ is the founder and director of The Village, a Jewish startup in Denver, Colorado, aiming at creating communities of connection surrounding infertility and new parenthood.

to programs specifically for them but, ideally, they would become part of the synagogue community: attending services weekly and other programming and, of course, becoming members. None of them joined the synagogue and most never even attended non-twenties/thirties events. Based on what seemed to be the goals or the synagogue and the donor, I felt like I had not been successful.

Yet, if I could go back in time and reframe my understanding of success, I would feel completely differently about the experience. If instead of focusing on numbers and connecting these twenty- and thirtysomethings to Jewish institutions, I would ask myself, "Each evening we were together, did we form a community?" to this question, I would have proudly answered, "Yes!"

Often community is thought of as something permanent or routine: our neighborhoods, which we have lived in for twenty years; our jobs, where we have worked collaboratively with the same people year in and out; and, ideally, our synagogues, where we go every week (or at least seasonally) to worship and for life-cycle events. But for Millennials, we don't have this same permanence. We are transient: frequently moving for new relationships, jobs, or interests. It's harder to feel a sense of community in a place where you have just moved. We tend to switch jobs every couple of years; not to mention, many of us work remotely and don't ever see our colleagues face-to-face without the help of the Internet. These factors coupled with competition in the workplace often leave little room for community. And though we might have fond memories of synagogues where we grew up, if we went to those spaces now, we likely would not know a soul, which feels more alienating than communal.

Millennials exist in a world of temporality: we get new cell phones every couple of years, we use these phones for apps like Snapchat, where the photos last only seconds, and we find out through Facebook about popup restaurants and galleries. So the idea of anything being permanent seems hard to relate to. Perhaps for Millennials, our sense of community is different. Perhaps, just like everything else in our lives, community is more temporal.

Fostering Temporary Communities

The word "community" comes from the Latin word *communis* meaning common. The prefix *com* means together, and *munis* means to fortify or strengthen. Thus, the word "community" means being strengthened together, a beautiful sentiment, but not one that necessarily implies permanence.

Being "strengthened together" definitely sounds like something Millennials would want given that our nomadic, technology-rich lifestyles often are very isolating. Not to mention that the American Psychological Association recently concluded that Millennials are the most stressed out generation.[2] This same report also documented how Millennials have the highest levels of feeling lonely and isolated.

So how do we as Jewish professionals foster temporary communities that provide the experience of being strengthened together? Places where you really feel like you belong, even if it is just for one night? Maybe you even feel like you've been there many times, even if you have never set foot in that space before?

One factor that is crucial is size. Though I felt guilty for only recruiting ten to fifteen people for our twenties/thirties Shabbat dinners, really the size was perfect because it was intimate. We think of a minyan as a minimum necessary for community, but when trying to create temporary communities, perhaps it should be the maximum. With about ten people, there were enough people that it felt substantial, but it was also small enough that we all learned one another's names. And we all had the opportunity to speak. It was a space where every voice at the table mattered.

Conversation, in particular, deep conversation, is another factor that is essential for creating temporary community. At the twenties/thirties dinners, a topic of discussion was announced prior to the dinner. Everyone who came knew beforehand that they were coming not just for food, not just to meet people, but also to have a conversation. Sometimes the conversation topics were more controversial, like talking about human rights violations in Israel. And yet even when the theme was talking about something more pareve, like Jewish communities in Central and South America, our conversation deepened and evolved to thinking about what it means to be a minority and what community feels like. It was in this conversation that one of the participants named these Shabbat dinners as his community.

My first experience where I felt part of a temporary community was at a lactation support group. Crammed into the lobby of a doctor's office, ten women, myself included, bared their breasts and their souls, sharing very deeply with complete strangers their fears and challenges. All of the women were having different challenges, but being in a room where I could hear that other people were struggling was so healing. I felt so much less alone. And hearing from the slightly more seasoned moms that they had experienced similar problems and had survived them gave me hope. By the end of the hour, I felt so close to these other women who had shared their stories with me. I have never seen any of them again and yet they all hold a very special place in my heart because of that one moment we shared together.

Where Are Millennials Finding Community and Where Aren't They Finding It?

Like so many Millennials, I turned outside of the Jewish world to find community and support.[3] Granted, I initially attended the lactation support group because of the physical challenges of breast feeding. But while there, I quickly realized that it was a space that I could not only get help with milk supply, but also where I could share my spiritual concerns. The lactation consultant was the one that invited this deep level of sharing by introducing the group with the line, "Please introduce yourself and the reason you are here this morning, and just wanting a place to go outside of the house is a great reason." That line stuck with me and I left the group vowing to return week after week because I had felt so nurtured in the space. Ultimately, I only went one other time when a different breast feeding issue came up. But even though I only participated those two times, they were two times that deeply impacted me. I always tell new moms about how helpful the lactation support group was for me, so that they too might experience it if they need help.

Following my experiences with the lactation support group, I thought about how held I felt in those two hours of my life as a new mom. Yet when it came to the organized Jewish activities I participated in routinely (synagogue, JCC programs and rabbinical school) I realized that none of these Jewish spaces were providing the same support or the same feeling of community as I had experienced those two times in the lactation support group. It occurred to me that as a new parent, I was experiencing some of my highest spiritual highs and my lowest spiritual lows, and I had not found a container in the Jewish community to help me delve into these moments.

This spiritual gap that I so longed to fill was the impetus for creating The Village, a Jewish startup I am working on thanks to a JTS grant from the Myers Family Foundation. The goal of The Village is to offer spiritually rich and supportive environments for two different demographics: new parents and people on a journey to parenthood who are struggling on this journey. I imagine that The Village will offer opportunities for these two groups to gather separately in small groups, max ten people. Jewish tradition and rituals will offer an anchor to ground people during these stressful and joyful life moments, but the bulk of the time together will be spent sharing deeply with one another. I pray that it will be a space where people are able to jump past the small talk and go straight to the many thoughts and fears that we are often too afraid to share with anyone else.

I like to say that The Village is currently in the "in utero" stage of development because I don't know exactly what will emerge. In order to build something that truly serves the Millennial demographic, I have spent the past four months having in-depth conversations with Millennial parents and Millennials who desperately want to become parents, and I have asked them to tell me stories about their spiritual life and parenting: how they have found support, what kind of support they would like, and where they have found community. Here are a few themes that have emerged:

For people who are struggling in any way, whether as a parent or as someone on a journey to parenthood, being around people going through the same thing is critical. These individuals shared with me how people who have not gone through a similar struggle often don't say the right thing and don't get how helpful it is to have another person around, even if it just means sitting quietly. One mom shared with me how she doesn't want to share her struggles as a parent with friends because so often people are struggling silently with infertility and she doesn't want to appear ungrateful for her children. Another mom, who recently experienced a death in her family and also became a caretaker for a parent, mentioned how hard it is for her to become friends with other parents because she feels like they all want to have very surface conversations, and she feels they are not available to handle the spiritual depths that she is living with. The majority of the parents and people on a journey to becoming parents that I have spoken with have not found this place where people in similar life stages can meet one another, share deeply, and be "strengthened together."

A few people have found community and spiritual support, both within and outside of the Jewish community. Jewish Baby University (JBU) is a birth and parenting class in the Denver/Boulder area with some Jewish content offered through the JCC and a local hospital. At times, though not always, the cohort of parents in JBU mesh into a community that exists after the class is over. One mom shared with me how she got together with women from her cohort on maternity leave once a week, just so she could get out of the house and be with women experiencing similar realities.

Many parents have found community through secular activities that they have participated in with their children. Stroller Strides, a fitness class where moms exercise with their child in the stroller, is one such place, as is Music Together, a class that brings families together to make music. Seeing the same people week after week at these classes and time spent after class schmoozing creates the opportunity for relationships to emerge. Other parents have found community online through websites like The Bump and Facebook groups for specific situations, like moms of high-needs children. Though many of these parents or people on a journey to parenting never meet face-to-face, they feel extremely close through having shared similar situations and very personal stories with their online community.

One religious organization that is devoted to building community and spiritually supporting moms with young children is MOPs (Mothers of Preschoolers). Although MOPs is a Christian organization, the biweekly program is not limited to participants who identify as Christian. In fact, one of the first people who mentioned MOPs to me was a Jewish dad. MOPs groups vary from chapter to chapter, but, in general, they meet in churches, offer childcare so that the mom gets some time for self-care, provide food, and offer a safe space at tables of six to eight women to, "laugh, cry and embrace the journey of motherhood."[4] This organization currently reaches one hundred thousand women a year nationally, 90 percent of whom fall within the Millennial demographic.

The Need for Community and Measuring Success with Millennials

These conversations have confirmed my suspicion that just like I felt desperate for a community of people going through similar situations, so are other Millennials. But these conversations have revealed that community can look different. Community might be routine, such as the same group that one gathers with weekly for Stroller Strides. But community might also be temporal, such as the Shabbat dinners I ran or the lactation support group I attended. Community might also be online. As Jewish professionals, we need to broaden our understanding of community when thinking about successfully engaging Millennials.

When thinking about the metrics I hope to use to measure the success of The Village, I hope to push myself beyond the standard questions of how many people are showing up, how many new versus repeat participants, and how many of them have become engaged with Jewish institutions. The first metric I will use will require stepping back after each gathering and just observing how the participants interact with each other. Are people talking to each other once the formal program has ended? Are phone numbers being exchanged? If so, I have successfully connected two people and perhaps have planted a seed for the organic growth of a relationship and maybe even the beginnings of a community that can exist independent of me. Following each Village gathering, I also plan to personally contact each participant. Thanks to having a max of ten people, it is doable to offer this individual attention, something I have found Millennials (myself included) long for. In this conversation, I plan to gauge if the gathering gave the individual meaning and a sense of community. Given my experience with how few people fill out surveys, I suspect getting authentic answers and a response is far more likely with a one-on-one conversation. Additionally, I hope to assess in this conversation if the participant found out about the program from someone else who had attended. Just like I only attended the lactation support group twice, certainly other Millennials will only attend The Village once or twice. If they are referring, though, it suggests to me that the one or two gatherings they attended provided them with meaning and with a temporary community—a temporary moment of being strengthened together.

Rabbi Chalafta teaches in *Pirkei Avot* that whenever ten people engage in the study of Torah the *Shechinah* is present among them. He then goes on to suggest that God is present even in smaller groups, even when there is only one person. As Jewish professionals, we are often pushed to create programs for as many people as possible. Our funders want to see big numbers and it can be hard to justify our time on just a few people. Yet, our work as Jewish professionals should be creating a space in which the Holy Presence dwells in our midst, and I would like to suggest that we can do this through bringing together intimate gatherings of people in similar life stages. Ideally, these spaces should be nurturing and also evocative so that the participants can vulnerably share the Torah of their lives. And, most importantly, if you find someone who is deeply searching for meaning, as many Millennials are, and they are not finding it, give them permission to seek outside of the Jewish world, and, if they find something that feeds their soul, give them the opportunity to create the meaning they are seeking within the Jewish world.

Notes

1. https://caspertk.files.wordpress.com/2015/04/how-we-gather.pdf.
2. http://www.apa.org/news/press/releases/stress/2014/stress-report.pdf.
3. Though not specifically about the Jewish community, see "How We Gather" by Casper ter Kuile and Angie Thurston, who document ways that Millennials make meaning in spaces outside of religious spaces.
4. http://www.mops.org.

"I Want You to Want Me": A Reflection on the Need for Obligation and Covenant

Sara Luria

"Julia, what are you feeling anxious about?," I asked at the first premarital session with Julia and Jon, an engaged couple in their late twenties. Julia responded as if she'd had this answer on the tip of her tongue for months, "I am nervous about having to take someone else into account when I make decisions."

Julia had spent her adult life thinking mostly of her own needs, her own career, her own dreams and now, she realized, she had to make space for Jon as they set out as committed partners on the journey ahead.

The recent report on Millennial engagement from the Jewish Federations of North America points to the very sentiment that Julia articulates, stating that, for Millennials, "their *personal experience* reigns . . . They are influenced by . . . the *freedom* that their life stage, emerging adulthood, brings them."[1]

Yet, Jon, also a Millennial, turned to Julia after hearing about her fears of sharing her life with him, and asked, "I know there are some things you will have to give up but you're also gaining such strong support. Don't you see how I support you?"

In the book of Hosea, God (in our story played by Jon), pleaded with Israel (Julia) to stop running after the false idols of temporary comfort and to remember what the covenant was actually about. *Israel! Julia! My love! Over here! I can promise you everything that is true and just and real in the world and, in return, promise to be mine always.*

Covenant is the only way.

SARA LURIA (NY13) is the founder and Executive Director of ImmerseNYC, a pluralistic, Jewish, feminist organization in New York City that facilitates deep ritual experiences, supportive peer communities, and educational programs.

In order to experience love, depth, and abiding, supportive community, we, progressive Jews, have to make a commitment. In our hyper-individualized age, we have to give up *some* autonomy in order to receive the connectedness we all need.

When reflecting on obligation, Rabbi Shai Held writes:

> Rashi explains that the priestly service "is a gift I have given to you" (comments to Numbers 18:7). Rashi's simple words are *subtly subversive of the ways we often think of responsibility and obligation*. Many of us find ourselves at times longing to be unencumbered—or at least *less* encumbered—by duties and obligations . . . In those moments, we tend to think of responsibility as an unbearable burden—and sometimes it is, in fact, just that. But the opposite extreme would be no better, and would likely be far worse: A life without responsibility would be a life devoid of meaning or purpose. Rashi's comment reminds us that obligation is a privilege. From a theological perspective, to be summoned to serve is an immense gift . . . a privilege, and a delight.[2]

At the bris of my youngest son, Judah, I felt like I was playing the part of "Jewish mother at son's bris." My stage directions included: furl brow, look worried, breathe heavily, wait miserably for it to just be over, express deep relief when it is. In this role, I felt connected to the Jewish women who have played this part for centuries and will play this part in the future.

I so reluctantly fulfilled this obligation, especially because I am not otherwise a halachically observant Jew. If the sign of the covenant were not so physically obvious, I surely would have skipped it, and we would have chanted some lovely prayers and skipped straight to bagels instead. A mother, vulnerable from childbirth, exhaustion, and overwhelming love, chooses the privilege of obligation, which means pain for her child.

Since the day evoked such strong, complex feelings of obligation for me, I was then particularly sensitive to those who felt obligated to be there—friends and family who traveled distances and rescheduled meetings to join this ritual. When you feel obligated to me, and I feel committed to this ancient ritual, the morning transforms from a snip followed by lox and herring into a unique moment in time, never to be repeated, in which we feel grateful knowing our lives have meaning because we are deeply obligated to each other.

Covenant is the only way.

If Millennials are willing to take this incredible leap of faith to be obligated to their communities and to the people in them, then the Jewish communities that they jump into *need to be there to hold them up.*

When Caleb, my oldest child, was a toddler, we went to our local synagogue for Tot Shabbat almost every week. We would sing and dance, I would try to sneak in some snippets of grownup conversation, and then we would grab a bagel and go home for our requisite Shabbat nap. When Caleb's baby sister, Eva, was born, Eva's nap coincided with Tot Shabbat, and I was just so tired on Shabbat morning anyway. I wondered, would anyone notice or care if I'm not at synagogue? The answer was no. I saw my friends and their kids at the playground in the afternoon instead and I just stopped going to shul.

I share this story not because I expected anyone from the synagogue to beg me to come back nor was there anything wrong with my particular local synagogue. *I share this story because I am asking you to ask me to stay.*

"I want you to want me; I need you to need me."

Fight for me as God did for God's people Israel in Hosea.

Obligate me the way my friends from two states away felt obligated to attend my son's bris.

Do not ask me just to set up *kiddush* or volunteer to run an annual cleanup day at the park. Ask me to share my unique gifts with you, to open my home, to make the sacrifices and compromises necessary to be a good partner to you, my community. And then support me, hold me up when my parents are getting divorced, or my child goes off to college, or I lose my job, or I experience a miscarriage. I will allow myself to be held but you need to promise to actually do the holding, just as Jon did for Julia on the precipice of their lifelong commitment.

Covenant is the only way.

NYU professor Marcia Pally beautifully illustrates this tug between obligation and independence in her book *Commonwealth and Covenant* by offering the understanding of "separability amid situatedness." She believes that:

> We want to go off and create and explore and experiment with new ways of thinking and living. But we also want to be situated —embedded in loving families and enveloping communities, thriving within a *healthy cultural infrastructure that provides us with*

values and goals . . . A contract protects interests, but a covenant protects relationships. A covenant exists between people who understand they are part of one another. It involves a vow to serve the relationship that is sealed by love.[3]

At *ImmerseNYC*, the organization I founded, we work to reimagine ritual experiences for our twenty-first-century Jewish communities. We have trained sixty-five people to be volunteer ritual facilitators—to listen to the needs, fears, and hopes of a person they just met; co-create a ritual with that person; and lovingly guide them through the ritual. Our ritual facilitators spend four days training to have the honor to guide these rituals, then some travel over an hour in the evening after work to be with a stranger who needs them. I often hear, "New Yorkers are busy!" Yet, our experience at ImmerseNYC is that we make time for experiences in which we can express love, feel needed, and deeply connect to ourselves and others. Maybe even through supporting and being supported, we can experience that which is transcendent.

Our *mikveh* guides feel needed because they are, in fact, crucial to the whole operation; our core program simply cannot happen without them. Most often, in the Jewish community, the responsibility to lead ritual is relegated solely to clergy. This means that only certain life-cycle events can be ritualized (there are only so many clergy and so many hours in the day) and that lay people are the passive recipients of ritual, not the active creators of sacred experiences.

Yet, covenant, as Pally describes, implies two active partners and a "vow *to serve* a relationship." Are we asking Millennial Jews to serve or just to show up? If more progressive Jews had access to serving their communities through leading ritual, they would have more ownership over their own personal Jewish lives and more confidence leading their peers. Additionally, more rituals could be created for a broader spectrum of life experiences. At ImmerseNYC, we call this work "spiritual leadership." An e-mail from a Millennial *mikveh* guide who had recently moved to New Jersey for graduate school exemplifies the virtuous cycle of spiritual leadership:

> I'm planning to do my best to get in to [Manhattan] for at least semi-regular guiding. It's been so sustaining for me. I had a conversation with [the ImmerseNYC program director] last night and tried to talk through what about guiding *mikveh* immersions

has been so good for me, and the most amazing thing is that I really feel like *I'm answering a call and have purpose, which is just exactly what I've needed.*

Clergy and educators can train their communities to facilitate sacred, creative rituals for themselves and their peers as one possible entry point for Millennial Jews to serve this covenantal relationship.

At ImmerseNYC, we have identified four principles that help us create and grow our covenantal community. These principles, which can be applied in a wide variety of contexts, are:

- **Active listening.** We listen for the deep underlying needs of the people in our communities and create space for their needs to be affirmed and, if possible, met.
- **Training.** We create engaging learning experiences in which people can cultivate their own inner teacher, develop confidence in a new skill, and begin to co-create the experiences they want/need.
- **Connectivity and support.** We connect people to each other and create environments in which they are held, supported, and loved by their peers and our staff.
- **Trust.** After listening, training, and connecting, we trust that those who commit to do the work will do the work, and we then commit to deeply valuing their contributions.

In my experiences thus far as a rabbi, I sense a Jewish communal hope that a few innovative programs or new initiatives will be the quick fix we need to engage the next generation. Yet, I believe this moment gives us the incredible opportunity to, as Pally suggests, *examine our cultural infrastructure.* Is our cultural infrastructure healthy? Is it flourishing? Are we teaching the Jewish values of love and interconnectedness in our synagogues, organizations, foundations, and communities? If not, why not? What values are we upholding through our current infrastructure? Why? Are we willing to make structural changes so that the Millennial generation that so values autonomy will willingly want to obligate themselves to a particular set of people, traditions, and rituals for the sake of meaning and connection?

May we all rise to this opportunity with open hearts and with the patience and courage that is always needed to uphold a covenant.

Notes

1. https://fedweb-assets.s3.amazonaws.com/fed-42/2173/JFNA_ Adults%2520Emerging_New%2520Paradigms%2520for% 2520Millennial%2520Engagement%2520Final.pdf.
2. https://www.mechonhadar.org/torah-resource/giving-taking-and-temptations-leadership.
3. http://www.nytimes.com/2016/04/05/opinion/how-covenants-make-us.html?_r=0.

Finding the Way to Friday

Jessica Minnen

Ten years ago I sat down at my first Shabbat dinner table. I was twenty-four and had just quit my job of two years in music journalism to take a "quarter-life crisis" trip to Israel to try to figure out what I wanted from this project called life. I spent the summer at the beach in Haifa, and at the university there I made friends who were about to head down to Jerusalem for the year. With little interest in returning to the States, I joined them.

That first weekend, a friend of a friend of a friend invited me to Shabbat dinner. Low on options, I accepted. I got dressed up. I navigated my way to their apartment, pre-GPS. I suppressed my nerves, and took a leap of, well, let's call it like it is: a leap of faith. And there they were, the happiest young people I had ever seen. I was shocked. I expected something boring; you know, like my memories of synagogue or Hebrew school. But here the joy was out of control.

I wanted to be happy too, but instead I sat there miserable. There was a lot of Hebrew going on. A lot of standing and sitting. Dish after delicious dish appeared from the kitchen, but I had contributed nothing. Then singing, and more singing. What were these kids on?

I excused myself to go to the bathroom and sat there, devastated. To make matters worse, there wasn't any toilet paper. Crisis. The tears welled up, and I buried my face in my hands and cried. And then something . . . shifted. I don't know why these transformational moments (at least for me) often happen in the bathroom. Perhaps it is because there we are at our most vulnerable and alone. This is a load of crap, I thought. Not my bathroom experience, but

---

JESSICA MINNEN (JTS13) is the Resident Rabbi at OneTable, a startup that helps people Shabbat together around the country, and the Founding Director of Seven Wells, which empowers participants in their 20s and 30s to explore the connection between spirituality and intimacy through the framework of Jewish text, values, and tradition.

the experience of not knowing, of feeling disenfranchised. I'm Jewish. This belongs to me as much as them. Why don't I know what is going on? It's not fair! Sadness turned to anger and I had my Scarlett O'Hara moment: "God as my witness," I said to the God I didn't believe in, "no one is ever going to feel this way again." And as I shook my fist, I turned and saw a pile of pre-torn toilet paper on the windowsill. Crisis averted.

Of course I didn't know then that keeping that promise would take me from Jerusalem to Stockholm, to graduate school in Baltimore, and ultimately to the rabbinate in New York. And I certainly couldn't have known that almost ten years to the day I made my bathroom oath I would join the founding team of OneTable, an initiative with a startling simple premise: sitting down with intention at the end of the week with food, wine, and friends is good for you. Period. Full stop. It's just a good idea, a good practice whether you're secular or religious, Jewish or not. Work is hard, relationships are complicated. You can't always change life. But on Friday night, you have the ability to change the way you engage with life.

I was born in 1981, which places me on the cusp of the Millennial generation. It was a big deal to have a pager when I was in high school, but by the time I was in college, Napster had changed the way we listened to music and texting had changed the way we made, kept, and, let's be honest, flaked on plans. Like never before, me and my friends turned to online social networks and peer-to-peer technologies to add value to our lives, to meet people, and to try new things. Yet we craved real life connection. We were turned off by institutions and sought instead grassroots ways to engage. Given the rapid pace of our daily lives, we actively carved out time to relax, and we loved nothing more than DIY details. So today, as a Jewish communal professional, it makes sense to return to Friday night, as it has always been a personalized Jewish space to slow down and enjoy time with the people who matter most.

OneTable was founded using the principles of Design Thinking, a user-centered methodology that requires understanding the barriers to participating in Shabbat dinner, both as a guest and a host. Even before getting to challenges around performing Jewish rituals in front of peers, hosts have other concerns. Building an enduring practice of Shabbat dinner runs counter to the instinct of emerging adults to try as many new things as possible rather than doing the same thing repeatedly. When Millennials come to OneTable, they seek guidance on what to serve, how to word their invitations, and reassurance that their friends will indeed come when invited.

For guests, OneTable competes with other social opportunities available to Millennials, who are often plagued by a fear of missing out. In our focus groups, emerging adults expressed concern that participating in Shabbat dinner might limit their other social options. We had to figure out how to make it as easy as possible for hosts and guests to create and attend Friday night dinners in a way that feels personally authentic and so compelling that they want to do it again and again. With the user at the center of our design process, we began to prototype and iterate.

The Shabbat dinner experience has to be accessible online, so all events are posted on OneTable's custom social dining platform (onetable.org), kind of like Airbnb for Friday night dinner. Most are intimate dinners hosted by individuals with eight to twelve guests. Guests report feeling more at home and more comfortable at smaller-scale dinners, and they provide an easier opportunity to meet new people than larger-scale events. Additionally, these smaller dinners lead more quickly to repeat Shabbat hosting or guesting practices. Our core programming is designed to empower hosts to create experiences that are welcoming and successful. To help hosts do just that, OneTable offers a range of support.

All hosts are eligible for Nourishment, an online credit valued at $15 per person, a maximum of $150 per dinner, that can be redeemed through web-based partners such as Instacart, Seamless, Drizly, or Etsy. We developed this resource in response to barriers to hosting such as lack of time, cooking skills, and financial constraints. Let's be clear: we are not paying people to have Shabbat dinner. Nourishment credit simply alleviates some of the stress of hosting and helps hosts plan ahead. (Dinners must be posted no later than Tuesday in order to receive Nourishment for Friday.) We also have a "Shabbat Hotline" staffed by our Community Specialist, who provides logistical support, including guidance on planning, cooking, and inviting, and advice on how to make the most of Nourishment.

But Nourishment isn't enough unless we're helping hosts develop the skills they need to host develop an enduring practice. So on a regular basis, hosts are invited with a +1 to attend "Nosh:pitality" gatherings. I designed these social workshops to be events I would actually want to go to with my friends. They are, for lack of a better word, cool. They take place at restaurants and bars and farms and co-working spaces. At Nosh events, our participants get a chance to reclaim the lost art of hospitality, to learn skills that will enhance their dinners, such as cooking, challah baking, cocktail mixing, and ritual facilitation. The gatherings also include integrated Jewish learning such as the role of wine at Shabbat dinner or a unique take on blessing the challah. Lastly, Nosh:pitality events create community among hosts and often result in new invitations to dinner.

In addition, hosts are matched with a mentor who takes them out for coffee or a beer and engages them in one-on-one Shabbat coaching. When we first started in the summer of 2014, I used to do all of the coaching. That was a lot of coffee. Today, I am (slightly) less caffeinated thanks to the coach training program we lead to scale coaching across the country in our anchor cities: New York, Chicago, San Francisco, Denver, and Washington, DC. The goal of coaching is to elevate hosts' thought processes about Shabbat dinner ritual. Coaches build personal relationships with hosts to help them develop skills and a sense of ownership. Coaches and hosts work together to design a personally meaningful set of Shabbat rituals for hosts and their guests.

Everything we do supports the development of a personalized Shabbat dinner practice. We continually refine our services, platform, and communications to ensure we are best empowering young adults to build their own micro-communities through Shabbat dinner. My role with OneTable has grown to include being our cities director. I am lucky to travel all over the country, supporting our regional staff and building unique, locally driven programs.

Most recently I was in Denver, our newest hub, supported by a generous grant from the Rose Community Foundation. OneTable Colorado is helping individuals weave a Shabbat practice into their lives by tapping into their search for new experiences. Colorado hosts want to integrate their pastimes and interests—from camping, to hiking, to going to concerts—into their Friday night practice. Unique dinners, like Shabbat dinners in the mountains with meals prepared over a campfire, have taken place. Also Shabbatot at Red Rocks and Phish parking lots before concerts, reflect the local culture. OneTable operates with a "bias toward action" and is always seeking to iterate and improve our program; this is true nationally. We've learned valuable lessons about our target population. For example, young Jewish Coloradans are often transplants from other places, and are seeking community in non-traditional ways. Our manager on the ground is already thinking about how the winter sports culture might impact Friday nights in the winter and is speaking with hosts about how an intimate and early Shabbat dinner can be a great way to kick off a weekend in the mountains.

Overall, for both hosts and guests, our data shows OneTable Shabbat dinners are mostly about time with friends, slowing down, and relaxing at the end of the week, where participants appreciate the Jewish tradition, connecting to their Jewish heritage and creating their own, unique Jewish community. Here's what some of them are saying:

> "Even though we can host a dinner any day of the week, Friday night dinner just makes it extra special and actually gives you that extra push to do something with friends at your own apartment." (OneTable Host)

> "It could have just been any other relaxing dinner with friends except that it clearly felt like a chance to make our own new Jewish traditions (very different than what each of our families grew up with, but still uniquely Jewish)." (OneTable Guest)

As resident rabbi, I remain focused on imagining how OneTable might not only create content but curate existing content in a way that invites the user, the dinner host or guest, to select based on his or her own interests the path that highlights the most useful content, be that dinner ritual, blessings, conceptualizing *hachnasat orchim* (the value of welcoming guests), and more. Our goal, rather than to assume what each host or guest might want to know, is to focus on user-centered design.

The Shabbat habit is catching on. OneTable now supports an average 1,000 seats at the table every Friday night. Entering 2016, we projected supporting 32,000 seats at the table (already aggressive growth over the 10,415 seats in 2015). We are now on pace to reach over 47,000 seats at the table in 38 cities.

For Millennials, OneTable presents a radical opportunity: become the active producer of your own Jewish experience, rather than passively consuming a Judaism produced for you. Empowering emerging adults to claim ownership of Jewish experiences that are self-made and personally authentic is a critical part of the shifting Jewish communal landscape, and at OneTable we are committed to supporting Millennials as they take the next step in their Jewish lives.

What began for me ten years ago as a transformational moment in the bathroom has become, thankfully, transformation at the dinner table. I don't mean to overstate the matter, but I believe that ending the week with an intentional meal can change the world. OneTable wants to share the joy of Friday night dinner practice not because we think it will make Millennials better, more confident, and more deeply engaged Jews, although it will. We want to share Shabbat dinner because I believe it will help Millennials become better, more confident, and more engaged human beings. And that makes for a better world.

Millenni-Y'all: Working with Jews in the South

Matthew Dreffin

When I moved to Jackson, Mississippi, to take my position at the Goldring/Woldernberg Institute of Southern Jewish Life (ISJL), I received the same question for three years and counting: why would you move from Los Angeles to Jackson?! I understand folks find it odd that I would willingly enter a land considered *b'midbar* in relation to the lush Jewish landscape of the Northeast, West Coast, or some other large cities. However, the South was, and continues to be, home. I found it necessary to do work that continues to support Jews who live in this region, not only because it contains a rich history, but also because it has a vibrant future.

Placing my work in context requires an understanding of the ISJL. The Institute started as the Museum of the Southern Jewish Experience. When parents would come to (then UAHC) Henry S. Jacobs Camp to drop their kids off, they brought Judaica and other items that were no longer in use. They wanted to preserve their community Torah or their Aunt Darleen's challah cover. The ISJL grew out of that situation and now looks to enrich the lives of Jews across a thirteen-state Southern region through our various departments: Museum, Cultural Programming, Community Engagement, History, Rabbinical, and Education. When the ISJL hired me it was with the caveat that I would split time between the Education and Rabbinical Departments, with the vast majority of my time spent in the Education Department. To quote one of my favorite songs about my favorite Southern city, "Well, I got one foot on the platform, the other foot on the train." My position in two departments gives me a unique experience working with a

---

MATTHEW DREFFIN, MAJE, (LA 13) is Associate Director for the Goldring/Woldenberg Institute of Southern Jewish Life (ISJL) in Jackson, MS

Millennial population in the field as a rabbi, as well as in the office as a supervisor of a team of recent college graduates.

Rabbinic Work in the South

I regularly travel on the road, although not quite as much as my colleague Rabbi Jeremy Simons. I drive to cities as close as Tupelo, Mississippi, and fly as far away as Blacksburg, Virginia. I only serve synagogues without full-time rabbinical leadership, which means I am going to smaller congregations (less than one hundred members), often without a huge population of Millennials or emerging adults. I lead services, programs, and, if I am lucky, interact with a religious school population.

There seems to be two main reasons that someone of the Millennial generation ends up in a small town with fewer socioeconomic opportunities (compared to legitimately metropolitan cities). The first reason to compel someone in the Millennial category to a place like Greenwood, Mississippi, is a family connection. When I visit towns with one synagogue composed of fewer than thirty members, you usually hear a story of emigration. The younger folks emigrated away when they got to college, never to return, and often "took" their parents with them when it was time to need some help with the newest family members (aka: kids had babies and now the grandparents want to be close). The family connection that brings someone back to these small towns usually requires taking over a family business or providing care for an ailing parent. Jewish Millennials of the small Southern towns choosing to live in their tiny hometown occurs infrequently compared to embedding themselves in the large cities.

The second compelling reason for someone from the Millennial generation to move to our small Southern towns is a reason a lot of us move anywhere: a job! There are a few particular professions that require an entry-level position in a small market. For example, I encountered a budding sports journalist who ended up in Selma, Alabama, and a fresh-out-of-school meteorologist who got a position in Charleston, South Carolina. The meteorologist already finished her two years and moved to South Florida. I suspect the sports reporter will dismiss the allure of the Selma Saints High School football team for a larger city with not only more young Jews (the president of Temple Mishkan Israel in Selma describes himself as the only one ambulatory enough to open the building), but more Jews (and sports) in general.

The bright spot in the South, regarding my likelihood of interacting with some teens and emerging adults of the Millennial generation, comes in small towns with colleges. Colleges seem to attract both students and professors who help buoy the Jewish residents of their municipalities. Universities like Auburn and Arkansas provide enough allure to keep a vibrant Jewish population afloat with new and exciting adventures. The grandest challenge I encounter is usually in the fall, when the leaves drop and the pigskin gets tossed in the great Southern stadiums. Contending with the religion of football is tough sledding; you cannot expect much participation in any part of the weekend, due to either competing events or a tiredness that accompanies daylong tailgates. But the presence of these institutions of higher learning provide ample opportunities for me to engage in one-on-one conversations over milkshakes, lead programs in fraternity houses, and have some folks who participate in my camp-style worship.

The one thing I have not been able to ascertain is how synagogues located near universities actively interact with their college population. Certainly, the communities say they are open to the students, with some shuls advertising that no one needs a ticket to enter any worship service. But, rarely do I see a congregation specifically trying to engage the students where they are. Instead, an attitude exists of "We will do what we want for us, and y'all can show up to our event." However, given my experience in larger environments, I am not sure this is an area in which bigger congregations excel. To be sure, there are folks in these small university towns who get to know their temporary members, inviting them into their homes, and always making sure there is a free meal for the "starving students."

The Education Department: A Millennial Population unto Itself

Currently, I co-supervise with our director of education, Rachel Stern, eight excited and enthusiastic recent college graduates who serve as itinerant educational consultants for our region. Each education fellow is assigned six to eight schools, of our current sixty-five, to act as an on-call educational consultant. What that means is assisting in the three Cs of our education program: curriculum, community, and conference. We lend to all of our partners a full set of our fully-scripted *curriculum*—Early Childhood through High School Judaics—to use for their religious schools. We do not just drop off the curriculum and say good luck; we consult throughout the year how to use it best for the congregation based on size, denomination, and a multitude of other factors. To help build the relationship between the fellow and the people in their congregations, they travel on three *community visits* per year—one in the summer, fall, and spring. They go for the weekend to lead services, run family programs, and bring a youthful excitement to Sunday mornings. The third C is an annual education *conference* that we run in Jackson, for which we require each community to send at least one representative. The fellows work on writing the curriculum, travel to all their communities, and plan every aspect of the conference throughout their two-year fellowship.

Because we have cohorts that overlap, we need to train and build a team every year in June. It caused me to alter my focus on personal professional development heavily. Instead of traditional Rabbinic sources like *Bava Batra* and *Arbaah Turim*, I've found my nose stuffed in books like *The Five Dysfunctions of a Team* and articles titled "11 Tips for Managing Millennials." Because my co-director and I care much more about being mentors than bosses, we spend a lot of time trying to get our department to function as one unit, rather than individuals, in the same office. By some numerical estimations, I am in the Millennial generation, but I recognize that I will continue to encounter a challenge. To paraphrase David Wooderson: I will get older . . . my staff will stay the same age. And that means I have to continue evolving my relationships with (and understanding of differences between) generations above and below me.

However, I can see some marked differences between my staff and I. For one, and this may come from being raised with a Southern respect for authority, I do not inherently have a need to challenge every rule I see as unfair or unwise. If, for example, we have a staff policy about showing up at a certain time, I may get challenged as to why it is necessary if all the work is getting done. My highly motivated and intelligent staff hears about their friends at a tech startup who can work from home or do not have to put in "regular hours," as long as they hit their deadlines. I am forced to explain to them how we work as a team, what it looks like symbolically when they decide for themselves that they can be late every day. Using what I learned in Bolman and Deal's four frames in *Reframing Organizations*, I think generations before the Millennial invasion had a higher emphasis on the structural frame. In other words, being their supervisor does not mean they will automatically begin the task I assign them. There may be a question of *why* are we doing this instead of just accepting the fact that a supervisor has said so. More often than not, Millennials are (unknowingly) operating out of the symbolic frame. They question moves we make because of how they think it looks or an interpreted meaning to the task.

What is interesting about their desire to question decisions is their wish for supervision. I do not mean lording over them, micromanaging every aspect of their lives. When either my co-director or I plan on being out of the office for any significant amount of time, our staff clamors, "What are we going to do?" I am not trying to self-aggrandize, but show that while we think all the pushback means Millennials think we are idiots, we also have a lot to offer them. It requires a lot of energy and training for them to be able to do their jobs properly, so I give them credit for jumping into the swimming pool of this job. For no matter how many classes they took in Jewish Studies or Organizational Studies, nothing can truly prepare them for the two-year grind we put them through. They have to program constantly, travel all over the South, and meet Jews with all sorts of accents they may have never encountered before. When they ask questions, sometimes it just means they want clarification and supervision, not necessarily that they think it is a mistake.

I have learned so much from my staff and continue to do so. I try to see things in perspective; while I wish that I could just say to them, "Go do this project," I have to understand that each question they ask regarding how to execute said project is an opportunity to develop and mentor someone towards their future. I try to give them the respect they deserve, for they are insanely smart with how much information they are able to balance and take in. Observing my staff as well as young Jackson socialites (forming a Moishe House Without Walls, for one thing), I've come to a couple of conclusions of how to work with and program for Jewish Millennials.

Lessons Learned

Be transparent, democratic, and inclusive. Being digital natives, Jewish Millennials in the South have had the ability to look things up insanely fast for most of their lives. Whereas we used to have to walk to the library, pick up a dictionary, and open the correct volume, this next generation can do it lightning fast. With a tap of their finger, they can fact-check virtually any statement in seconds. Furthermore, they have accessed a greater swath of cultures and people than we ever thought imaginable twenty years ago. For that reason, they do not see boundaries the same way previous generations conceived them. If you are planning an event, you cannot restrict it to "just Jews," because the Millennial generation wants to invite everyone to the table. Through this multitude of voices, they feel they can have the best experience possible.

Create clear boundaries and (multiple) deadlines. Ambiguity seems to be a source of frustration when it comes to the working environment. Instead of seeing an amorphous set of instructions as an opportunity to play within the rules, Millennials find themselves paralyzed (or unwilling to put forth full effort). The reason for this is that they feel like they do not know exactly what I, as their supervisor, want, so why try 100 percent? Instead, they will turn it in partially completed to get feedback and a better understanding of what truly "done" means. Furthermore, big projects need broken-up deadlines, not a singular end date. We cannot expect to say, "Curriculum needs to be done by April 1," especially if they do not know what that process looks like. With clear boundaries and (multiple) deadlines, my staff and I get more done with less consternation on both sides.

Location, location, location. For thousands of years, the synagogue building has been the central hub of Jewish life. Congregants felt a sense of obligation. However, Millennials do not necessarily feel the same way. I am always impressed when someone between the ages of thirteen and thirty is in shul on Friday night when I travel. Instead, try to figure out how to latch on to cultural events that are happening in the greater community. You cannot expect young Jews who just moved to a city to come to a synagogue simply out of a connection to their heritage. But, you can meet them at a Celtic Fest or Dragon Boat Regatta. Figure out how to set up a delegation to connect with them, and their non-Jewish friends, simply to hang out and get to know one another without ulterior motives (read: signing up for synagogue membership). The same goes for working in the office. Like that college class that went outside for gorgeous weather, a change of location for work can be invigorating.

Remember what it was like to be at this stage in life. Sometimes we look down on Millennials for not being mature enough, while other times we expect too much out of them. When we find ourselves thumbing our nose at this generation, we should take pause to remember this has happened for centuries. Remember how Jim Stark's parents seemed so confused by him in *Rebel Without a Cause*? Take the time to get to know individuals in this generation and not write them off as a singular unit. It will help us in all aspects of our life.

Israel: A Diaspora Dialogue

Hannah Ellenson and Jacqueline Koch Ellenson

Introduction

As mother and daughter, Israel is woven into the heart of our relationship. And in many ways, we have had parallel stories of love, connection, disappointment, and return. We do not have the same story, though. Our generational difference parallels our different experiences and perspectives of Israel. Our family has never shied away from discussing Israel, even in the moments when we do not agree. Whether or not to sing "Hatikvah" has become a flash point at the end of each year's seder. But that we can have that conversation and feel so strongly about it is what this piece is about. We both ultimately agree that in order to feel connected to Israel, one must be able to explore all parts of it—both the easy and hard. Through our own stories, we hope you understand the deep trust we have of each other, the commitment we have to Israel, our continued shared engagement, and the desire for Israel to be a place we can love.

Jackie

I fell in love quickly. It happened on the first day. And no matter what, I am still in love. But like everything and everyone we fall in love with, that love becomes tempered over time as we learn more and live with the day-to-day reality. Love seems to come before knowledge. And knowledge can sometimes take away the love.

On my first visit to Israel, as a wide-eyed sixteen-year-old, I immediately felt as though I had come home. My grandmother

---

HANNAH ELLENSON is the Associate Director of the San Francisco Region and Board Liaison at the New Israel Fund and a member of If Not Now. She received her Masters in Public Policy in Conflict Resolution and Mediation from Tel Aviv University.

JACQUELINE KOCH ELLENSON (NY83) is the Director Emerita of the Women's Rabbinic Network. Her communal commitments focus on religious pluralism and women's empowerment in Israel and North America. She is currently working in the field of adult spiritual formation, as a teacher and spiritual director, in New York City.

brought me to Israel to celebrate my birthday, and we spent ten days touring the country. Even as a person raised in the very ethnic and Jewishly inflected Upper West Side of Manhattan, I had never ever felt the intensity of belonging and connection I experienced that week. The first morning I woke up to watch the sunrise over the Judean Hills. That light entered into my heart and from that moment on, I knew that Israel was truly my home. I decided I would study Hebrew in college and I would definitely come back.

Looking back at that sixteen-year-old version of myself, I envy her love of the State of Israel. I don't envy her lack of Jewish knowledge. But I envy the purity of the experience, unsullied by reality, unaware of Palestinians and war, believing that we as Jews had a right to live in the State of Israel and to protect and defend her borders. As time has passed, I realized that the Israel with which I fell in love—pictures of Israelis dancing the hora in my mind—that Israel no longer existed, and perhaps never had. As I became more knowledgeable and aware of the realities of the country, with more friends living the realities there, David and I raised our children and wondered how we would convey our commitment to and love of Israel.

We wanted our kids to love Israel as we had, to experience the country with a sense of home we had both experienced. So when David had the chance to go to Israel for a yearlong sabbatical, we jumped and took our three younger children there for the year. We imagined this time would profoundly impact our children, instilling in them the deep love we felt, giving to them the same unshakable commitment to Israel as we possessed—and, who knew, perhaps one day our kids would make *aliyah*!

Now almost twenty years later, that year seems like a dream. It most definitely wasn't. It was challenging beyond all expectations. We were Americans living in a Middle Eastern country. Our daughters and I were miserable for the first three to four months. We lived in French Hill, in the northern part of Jerusalem. It is immediately adjacent to Isawiyyah, a large Arab town. We couldn't drive home without driving through East Jerusalem and Sheikh Jarrah. I could see the differences in housing and access to services in the Jewish and non-Jewish neighborhoods. Within the first month of our stay, there was a horrific bombing in the center of Jerusalem. My best friend's son was visiting; I knew that he had planned to go downtown that day, and I was petrified. I could not breathe until I finally, thankfully, found out that he was safe, but other people's children were not. We didn't go downtown for quite some time after that. But our life, for the most part, proceeded in a bubble. It was a bubble we tried to maintain as we confronted the sad reality of the senseless deaths of so many, Israelis and Palestinians, and protected ourselves from feelings of frustration and disappointment about the ongoing struggle for peace.

Slowly over the course of that year, we wove connections to people, which remain strong to this day. The day we left Israel to return home, all of us were in tears, sobbing loudly as we said good-bye to the many friends we had made. We succeeded in having, and giving to our children, a profound, life-transforming experience. We left feeling we belonged, that Israel was our home, and that we had a part to play in this enterprise, even if we were returning to Los Angeles. Our goals may have been unrealistic. In the aftermath, all of them have a strong connection to Israel, but in ways that I couldn't have imagined while we were there.

In the years that have passed since then, our children have become adults. All five of them are interesting and engaged in many different things, open to life and eager learners. They also have become adults with their own ideas about Israel. Hannah, my daughter and coauthor, is employed by a nonprofit that invests in peace building, religious pluralism, and the creation of a civil society in Israel. I want Hannah to love Israel. But she doesn't and can't love Israel as I did as a young adult. Her Israel is very complicated and complex, riven with cultural, religious, and economic divides. Her Israel is equally responsible for the lack of peace and the inability to create a Palestinian state. Her Israel is judged for committing war crimes. I'm sad that this is the Israel with which she has grown up.

But I also don't love Israel as I did as a young adult. No longer can I live in a bubble. Whether I am in Israel or at home in New York, I am always aware of what is going on there. In response, I have developed my own commitment to Israel advocacy, in the arenas of religious pluralism and women's rights and empowerment. I stand alongside my sisters of Women of the Wall when they are jeered and screamed at, when they absorb the impact of thrown objects or are detained in police stations for the "crimes" of daring to believe that women and men should have the right to pray out loud at the Western Wall. I cringe when the government announces yet another round of settlement building in the West Bank. I was challenged to my core when I visited a Palestinian refugee camp. I still shiver when I relive the experience of that rainy cold day, seeing first hand how dispossessed Palestinians have lived since 1967. I am devastated over and over each time the government takes another action to deny financial and spiritual support to emerging non-Orthodox communities while doing everything they can to strengthen ultra-Orthodox institutions.

The Israel in which these situations exist is a very hard Israel to love. That Israel brings me to tears of anger and frustration. I don't love that Israel. So how can I expect that Hannah would? My formative experiences took place during a time of relative calm. I was in Jerusalem when Anwar Sadat visited. We were in Israel the summer after the Oslo Accords had been signed. I had within me the faith that Israel could find a way through the morass of fighting wars to create a country that enabled the coexistence of two peoples next to each other. My children's formative experiences, of bus bombings and Rabin's assassination, hold no such thing.

This has led to some extremely challenging conversations among us in recent years. The alphabet soup of historical Zionist organizations, AIPAC and JNF, is now considerably impacted by the presence of J Street, Jewish Voices for Peace, and the BDS movement. Even a seemingly simple act of considering the purchase of a Soda Stream seltzer maker was very contentious. Our kids see Birthright as the equivalent of taking young adults to a Jewish Disneyland, "protecting" them from any awareness of the realities that Israelis and Palestinians confront on a daily basis.

On one hand, I feel a deep sense of loss on Hannah's behalf. She will never have the same naïve and pure love I had when I was her age. She will never experience the high of knowing deeply that Israel is her home and homeland, nor will she ever have an unambivalent response to the idea of a Jewish homeland. Her Israel will never be seen without an uncritical eye. Sometimes I even feel disappointed in her views. I wish she could see what I saw, feel what I felt, believe what I believed. My Zionism is not her Zionism, and frankly, I'm not even sure she would identify with that label.

But on the other hand, I am proud of her struggle. She has had to work much harder than I have to maintain a connection and a commitment. She takes nothing for granted. Hannah looks with critical eyes but also commits to not look away. She lives with an Israel that is both under attack, physically and internationally, and the Israel that is also the quintessential "start-up nation." Hers is an intentional decision to remain in the conversation and to not walk away. Hannah knows that if Israel is to change, she has to be a part of the work. She has to maintain her commitment to the country, even as she may support organizations and activities that I reject. I may perceive her commitments as contradicting everything I've ever thought and believed. But she sees them as affirmation of her deepest faith in Israel, and as an expression of her aspiration for the Israel that could be.

Maybe this pure love that I yearn for nostalgically isn't really the goal. Maybe the Israel of Leon Uris's *Exodus* shouldn't be the Israel I want and need my children to believe in. In any case, it can't be. I want them to love Israel, the state, the country, and its people. I am grappling with the possibility that Hannah's activism allows and enables her to have, perhaps not a pure love for the country, but a mature love; one that sees Israel for its missteps and mistakes, its achievements and successes—to see it as it really is, with all of the complications, warts and all. Hannah has found her own way to love Israel, but it reflects a deeper awareness and capacity to hold the contradictions. I have learned from her that pro-Israel activism casts a wide net. It allows us to act on our Jewish, democratic and pluralistic values; these values give us a voice; and help us feel more connected. There is more than one way to be a Jew and there is definitely more than one way to love Israel.

My children won't have the love or surety I had, but they will have something stronger, something that can thrive, is nimble and responsive to the changes taking place in Israeli society today. It's my responsibility to find a way to understand the Israel they love and to understand how they express that love. I may have worried that their commitment to Israel was weak and too critical. Now I see that their dedication comes from serious soul-searching and confrontation with their values and actual facts. I wanted Hannah and her siblings to find their own paths to loving Israel and assuming responsibility for Israel's existence and future. And with their own eyes, the eyes of mature and seasoned people, they do.

Hannah

While I like to think of myself as an individual (a Millennial trait), I fit perfectly into the young adult community that Peter Beinart described in his now infamous article, "The Failure of the American Jewish Establishment."[1] As I have learned more about Israel, I have grown more wary and distrusting of the Israeli government and I want to see Israeli policy, particularly as it relates to the Palestinian people, change. The values I was raised to promote of social justice, democracy, and religious pluralism seem oftentimes to be at odds with what Israel is doing: occupying another people, not having a clear separation of church—or in this case, synagogue—and state, and confronting very real threats to its democratic nature as one piece of legislation after another is passed thought the Knesset that further restrict NGOs' ability to work or artists to speak out against settlements.

Most of my close friends are engaged with Israel in one way or another, but that is not a representative sample set of my generation. I see far more of my peers, even some of whom that are involved with the Jewish community, saying that Israel is too hard, too complicated, too sad for them to want to stay engaged with it. I have not taken that path. As the daughter of two rabbis, one could attribute that to the way I was raised, but I think that is a simplistic understanding. My work has encouraged me to hold Israel so close that not only do I see its warts, but I also see the people who are working to make it better every day. I do not want to turn away from Israel, nor do I think I would be able to if I tried; I want to bring it closer.

I was nine the first time I felt truly connected to Israel. Of course, even before that, I had heard countless stories about my grandmother's Hadassah involvement and my dad's time picking oranges on a kibbutz, and I was learning about Israel in my Jewish day school, but I did not understand why there needed to be a country so far away that I was supposed to love.

On November 4, 1995, Prime Minister Yitzhak Rabin was assassinated. The following day, my parents took us to a memorial rally in front of the Israeli Embassy on Wilshire Boulevard in Los Angeles. Perhaps this is an odd place to bring a child, but I am so glad they did. There were thousands of people there, and the street was closed off to accommodate everyone. I understood for the first time that what happened in Israel affected me deeply here, and even more than that, what I did here affected people in Israel. I remember that feeling of finally understanding that connection everyone had been talking about—that this is what it means to be part of *Am Yisrael*.

I like to say that even though I did not grow up in Israel, I did a lot of growing up in Israel. My parents wanted us to feel connected to this place that was so far away, so we went for a year on sabbatical when I was in sixth grade. I attended an Israeli school, made friends, and learned more Hebrew in a day than I could have possibly learned in a month at my school in Los Angeles. The beginning of the year was incredibly difficult, but at some point a few months later, it not only became easier, but I also felt at home. I was heartbroken when we left at the end of the school year. On the way to the airport, I sobbed in the back seat of a taxi sitting next to my Abba as he cried, too.

Returning there every summer for the next several years further solidified my connection to Israel as I attended summer camp with Israelis, reconnected with friends, and spent time with my family in this place we all loved. The summer before my senior year of high school, I attended a program in New York organized by Auburn Theological Seminary for teenagers from Northern Ireland, South Africa, the United States, and, yes, Israel and Palestine. I had seen Palestinians before (I have a clear memory of the gardener who would wave at me on my way to school in Jerusalem and knowing that he was different than me, and we often drove through Palestinian neighborhoods to get places), but this was the first time I had the opportunity to actually speak to a Palestinian. I'm sure it was no coincidence that the girl who shared my bunk bed was from a small Palestinian town outside of Jerusalem.

We spent our days learning how to truly listen to and empathize with each other, and talking about that which would normally divide us: gender, religion, class, and political beliefs. This was the first time I ever heard the IDF described in anything less than heroic terms, and I heard stories from my new friends of what Israel had done to their neighborhoods, families, and schools. I was again heartbroken, but this time it was not because I was leaving a place that had become home. I did not want to think of Israel as anything less than perfect, as a light unto the nations. I had an incredibly difficult time listening and not thinking of my next point to prove them wrong. Over the next few weeks, though, I began to change my perspective and be more open to hearing the stories of those around me. I was not done with Israel, but I was acknowledging that the political situalion in Israel needed to shift significantly.

Reflecting on this moment now, I feel deep shame. How had I, a product of Jewish day schools and camps in the United States and Israel, never heard anything other than stories of perfection, stories of *chalutzim* tilling the soil and draining swamps, stories of Palestinians being the only ones that were wrong? Had I missed that day in school where a more complex narrative was shared?

I returned to Israel many times during college, including a semester abroad at Hebrew University in Jerusalem. I spent most of my time that semester with Palestinian friends in East Jerusalem. As soon as I returned to the United States, I was determined to go back to invest in Israeli society so that I could no longer be dismissed as the young American woman who had no real stake in the future of this country. I wanted to affect social change and work with activists to promote values of social justice and civil rights for all. I was growing more uneasy with Israeli governmental policies and what I saw as clear threats to Israel's democratic character. During this period, talking about Israel with my parents became increasingly challenging, and there were a number of occasions where we had to stop conversations before they even started to avoid arguing.

By the time I went back to Israel after college, I was growing more comfortable with the dualities I was holding. I loved living in Israel—the culture, the food, the language—and I was also critical of the political situation. On Fridays, I would often go from my apartment in Tel Aviv to the West Bank to help a Palestinian farmer harvest olives or plant trees or to a demonstration in the neighborhood of Sheikh Jarrah in Jerusalem to protest Palestinian expulsion by Jews, followed by *Kabbalat Shabbat* services and dinner with friends. There were few people who were doing both, but I did not know how else I, someone with immense privilege in Israel, could spend my time any other way. On one of these days, a friend met up with me and we sat outside overlooking the walls of the Old City. She was in utter disbelief that this was what I would choose to do, and yet, in the same breath said, "We need you here."

I ultimately decided I did not want to stay in Israel—everything started to feel too hard. I could not justify becoming a citizen of a country where my friends had been born and were not given the privilege of citizenship. My parents' friends who had made *aliyah* in the 1970s, admitted they never expected to be sending their children to the army so many years later. I did not want to have that same future. I know my parents were happy to have me come back to the United States and also a little disappointed that I had not fulfilled the dream of *aliyah*.

Now, several years later, I am confident with the decision I have made to live my life in the United States. My work keeps me connected to Israel every day and I feel incredibly lucky to feel so close to what happens there. And I will always wonder about what would have happened if I had stayed.

While I was living in Tel Aviv, my parents came to visit. While walking around the mall in Dizengoff Center, I told my mom how glad I was to not know where home really was—Israel or America—because we had always gone back and forth so much and I spoke the language of both, although I was not a true Israeli. She cried and apologized to me; she wanted me to feel at home in one place and not have the constant pull of two countries. Now, years later, I am still glad to have the opportunity to wrestle with my connection to Israel. I would not have it any other way.

Note

1. http://www.nybooks.com/articles/2010/06/10/failure-american-jewish-establishment/.

Millennial Responsa

The Meaning of Life
An Intergenerational Literary Conversation among Max Fitzgerald, Rabbi Amanda Greene, and Rabbi Seth Limmer (Chicago Sinai)

Amanda Greene and Seth Limmer

Max Fitzgerald

Growing up, Judaism was the ritual of going to religious school three times a week and participating in Shabbat most Friday nights. Religion was more responsibility woven into our family's weekly calendar than a spiritual connection. After graduating from college, I helped care for an ailing father who ultimately died when I was twenty-seven. During those years my connection to Judaism was mostly appeasing my mom by attending High Holy Day services with her or being home for the seders at Passover. While I never lost my belief in God, my faith was tested upon my dad's death as I seemed empty and spiritually aimless. It was only after saying *Kaddish* at my dad's first *yahrzeit* that I realized how important my community was to me, and suddenly I was energized to renew my relationship outside of perceived obligation. While Millennials today are probably less "religious" by ritualistic standards, many still want to be part of their faith communities. Jews have always seemingly questioned the status quo; heck we wouldn't have the Talmud without the mentality, so how can we use this core value to connect with a generation known for not being satisfied with

---

AMANDA GREENE (LA15) is the assistant rabbi of Chicago Sinai Congregation of Chicago, IL.

SETH LIMMER, DHL (NY00) is the senior rabbi of Chicago Sinai Congregation of Chicago, IL, the Chair of the Justice, Peace and Civil Liberties committee of the Central Conference of American Rabbis, and as Vice-Chair of the Commission on Social Action of the Union for Reform Judaism

explanations at face value? How can modern Judaism bring back meaning to a world so connected, yet so impersonal?

Rabbi Amanda Greene

I have often been criticized for not caring about religion. Well, not me personally, but my generation, the infamous Millennials. When the Pew Research Center in 2014 released their most recent study on religion, the fear of religious groups losing contact with Millennials grew dramatically. Two years later, people still ask me, "So what is it about your generation that makes you indifferent to religion?"

Max's experience demonstrates perfectly the answer I give every single time: Millennials DO care. They care about spiritual life in general, and Judaism in particular. They actively seek meaning in their lives. They strongly yearn for connection to other Jews and to their religious community.

The question Max poses is an important one, although perhaps it represents the reason our generation gets the reputation for being disengaged or even worse, simply not caring about Judaism. Max has accurately depicted our Jewish tradition as one that continues to question the status quo. As a Millennial, he also experiences himself—and this resonance we would be foolhardy to ignore—as one who constantly questions the status quo. Max and his peers are not a generation who simply do things because they are told to do them or because a previous generation found them meaningful. The details of the status quo have no special priority; it is mostly the privileged position of challenging the status quo that makes Judaism so appealing. Thus Max asks how we can use this very method of questioning the status quo to engage Millennials.

Here are a few standard assumptions I continue to question:

Status Quo: **Synagogues want young professionals to become dues-paying members.**

I have found that young professionals are more willing to meet with me when I share with them that I am not trying to get them to become a member or join a synagogue. In other words, I begin my encounters by being forthright in questioning the status quo. When I share this with the young professionals, I tend to hear a sigh of relief and, often immediately after that, a willingness to open up and share their story.

Status Quo: **Jewish professionals have to do all the legwork.**

We are no longer dealing with religious school: parents can't force their adult children to attend. However, when these same adults plan the events, they become invested. At my first leadership team meeting, people talked about wanting a place to do social action. Two people on the committee organized an evening of cooking a meal at a homeless shelter. Within only a few hours, the sign-up list was full. As the rabbi, I did not need to convince anyone to come. I wasn't begging my peers to come to Friday Night Services or to a Sunday morning program at the synagogue. They wanted to volunteer, they planned it, and they showed up. And, in time, they brought their friends, too.

Status Quo: **The Synagogue is the center of Jewish life.**

The memories of boring Shabbat services, or long High Holy Days, or dreadful Sunday mornings steer young professionals away from the synagogue. Where does this generation like to go? Yoga, SoulCycle, the local beer garden, friends' homes, sporting events. So I meet them there. But I bring my Jewish content with me. When attending a Cubs game, we made sure to buy tickets and sit in the Autism Awareness section. We met the young adult who brought out the score cards, and he sat with us while he shared his experience with the organization and expressed his gratitude for our support. We celebrated Shabbat and studied Jewish texts in a private room at a bar. When people left, they went out for dinner with friends and posted photos on Facebook, capturing their Friday night out with, "Shabbat Shalom." Recognizing that there are different cohorts of people in their twenties and thirties, we hosted a *Havdalah* at the senior rabbi's home for newly married couples. The evening provided an opportunity for young couples to meet one another, share their stories and experiences as newlyweds, and reconnect informally with the rabbis who officiated their wedding ceremonies.

Status Quo: **Millennials won't step foot inside a synagogue.**

When I ran out of options for a location for a challah baking event, I turned our office-like rabbinic suite into the communal feel of a family room or kitchen. People who had walked by the synagogue hundreds of times finally walked in the mysterious building they knew was always there. Once in the building they asked when services were and asked about how to get involved in various areas of congregational life that interested them. We've hosted a few other events at the synagogue, and I can already see it starting to feel like home—they know their way around. Because they came on their own terms, they are the ones deciding to make it their home.

Status Quo: We are talking about outsiders.

No. we are talking about ourselves! I'm a twenty-nine-year-old woman, was in a sorority in college, and grew up on the North Shore of Chicago. I like deep dish pizza, I like to go to the bar after work for a drink . . . and yes I'm also a rabbi. I wore jeans to the Cubs game and got messy when we baked challah. I write "Amanda" on my name tag. I don't keep kosher, and I celebrate Shabbat by having dinner with friends at a restaurant after services on Friday night. But I'm still a rabbi. Perhaps this is the best example of "questioning the status quo." I'm not the picture of a "perfect" or "religious" or "super" Jew that so many young professionals have in the mind when they think "rabbi." I'm a twenty-nine-year-old who connects to Judaism and finds it meaningful and wants to share that potential for meaning with others.

What Millennials seek is actually no different from what any generation seeks—connection. Max's second question asks: how can Judaism bring meaning into a world that on the one hand seems so connected and on the other, so impersonal?

What brought Max back to Judaism was his experience reciting the Mourner's *Kaddish* on his father's first *yahrzeit*. What Max did not write, but what I am certain did happen that day, was that he recited the *Kaddish* amongst a congregation, within a community. He was not alone.

The answer to Max's second question is summed up in a simple Hebrew phrase: *panim el panim*. By bringing Jews together, face to face, they create real relationships that lead to meaningful connections. They help each other navigate the working world, share insights into wedding planning or purchasing their first homes. I've quickly learned that it doesn't matter how many people are in the room if no one is talking with one another. Rather, it is the depth of the relationships, of the rituals, of the experiences that begins to question the status quo and provide meaning. In a world where we are all so connected by technology or impersonal relationships, Judaism reminds us that even Millennials, when we encounter an other, *panim el panim*, bring the presence of the Divine into our world.

Rabbi Seth M. Limmer

I love being part of this conversation. And I love that this conversation is happening publicly. To me, this is the colloquy we imagine has been taking place since the very beginnings of our Jewish story. This discussion started millennia ago in Mesopotamia:

Haran died in the presence of his father Terah (Gen. 11:28).
Rav Hiyya said: Terah was a manufacturer of idols. He once went away somewhere and left Abraham to sell them in his place. A man came and wished to buy one. "How old are you?" Abraham asked him. "Fifty years," was the reply. "Woe to such a man!" he exclaimed, "You are fifty years old and would worship a day-old object!" At this [the old man] became ashamed and departed.
. . . On another occasion a woman came with a plateful of flour and requested him, "Take this and offer it to them." So he took a stick, shattered them, and put the stick in the hand of the largest. When his father returned, he demanded, "What have you done to them?" "I cannot conceal it from you," he rejoined. "A woman came with a plateful of fine meal and requested me to offer it to them. One claimed, 'I must eat first,' while another claimed, 'I must eat first.' Thereupon the largest arose, took the stick, and shattered the rest." "Why do you make sport of me," he cried out, "Do they have any knowledge!" "Let your ears listen to what your mouth is saying!" Abraham retorted.
Immediately Terah seized him and delivered him to Nimrod.
"Let us worship the fire," [Nimrod] proposed.
"Let us rather worship water, which extinguishes the fire," [Abraham] replied.
"Then let us worship water!"
"Let us rather worship the clouds which bear the water."
"Then let us worship the clouds!"
"Let us rather worship the winds which disperse the clouds."
"Then let us worship the wind!"
"Let us rather worship human beings, who withstand the wind."
"You are just bandying words," he exclaimed. "We will worship naught but the fire. Behold, I will cast you into it, and let your God whom you adore come and save you from it." Now

Haran was standing there undecided. If Abram is victorious, [thought he], I will say that I am of Abram's belief, while if Nimrod is victorious I will say that I am on Nimrod's side. When Abram descended into the fiery furnace and was saved, he [Nimrod] asked him, "Of whose belief are you?" "Of Abram's," he replied. Thereupon he seized and cast him into the fire; his inwards were scorched and he died in his father's presence. Hence it is written: *Haran died in the presence of his father Terah.*[1]

Our Midrash captures the iconoclasm—and more—embedded in our Millennial dialogue. But this goes well beyond Abraham literally smashing his father's idols; the nuances of the narrative capture so much more. First, the father makes the mistake of imagining his son inherited his belief: Terah falsely assumes his son was as committed to his faith as he was, equally invested in idolatry. Terah only realizes his mistake when his son—in a line of dialogue and fit of exasperation fitting for any coming-of-age movie—challenges him with the words, "Let your ears listen to what your mouth is saying!" Since the start, Jewish children have tested the assumptions, the faith, and the practice of their parents. This is the brilliance of Rabbi Greene lining up so many of our assumptions, only to smash them and place new ideas in their place. It remains remarkably Jewish for the coming generation to upend the standards of the status quo.

Beneath the commitment to questioning is the continuing journey of religious development. Before smashing any idols, Abraham only discourages others from placing their faith in material objects. After arguing with his father, Abraham enters into more philosophical speculation in his debate with King Nimrod. Abraham proceeds from a stage of inquiry—how could a man your age worship this idol fabricated yesterday?—through a revolutionary overturning of inherited systems, and he ultimately comes to defend the beliefs he developed through his struggles. This is not so dissimilar from Max's evolution of his connection, disconnect, and reconnection with Jewish thought, practice, and community. The assumptions of Max's childhood were challenged, and it took time for him to arrive at the place where he opted not only to participate in our congregational life, but also this rather public discussion. We would do well to remember that even the titans of our patriarchal past took time to grow into the fullness of their Jewish commitment.

Then there is Haran. Standing on the side. Uncertain. A simple sacrifice of our Jewish narrative: with a few words, we dispense of Haran, his story, his struggle. It literally consumes him. He is no more part of our Jewish story. The stringency of societal expectations embodied by Nimrod, the pious assuredness of Abraham, and the mistaken insistence of Terah all combined to sideline Haran eternally from our Jewish story. How sadly reminiscent of all those today who are departing forever from Jewish life. Sadder still that we do not assume responsibility for our roles in making the modern-day Haran the accidental sacrifice of contemporary times. If only we would step up and save him from the sometimes consuming fires that are perceived societal and synagogal expectations.

Lastly, there is longing. In keeping with the search for community both Max and Rabbi Greene capture, the deep despondency of our ancient midrash is that son longs to connect with father, father with son, brother with brother, neighbor with neighbor, each with a community *that understands them*. Our midrash preaches precisely what Rabbi Greene and Max explain: we will only be able to build interconnected communities of meaning when we allow our assumptions to be challenged. Max wants to question the face value of inherited assumption *and* is seeking connection in a world often impersonal. Rabbi Greene reminds us of the primacy of *panim-el-panim* interpersonal relationships but also knows that we need to recast the settings where those connections are forged. Just as she concludes her essay with the import of bringing the Divine Presence into our world, so too do our stories—from Max to the midrash—remind us of our obligation to create places for Millennials to be present in vibrant Jewish life.

Note

1. *Midrash B'reishit Rabbah* 38:13. Translation is my own.

Innovative Tradition
An Intergenerational Literary Conversation among Risa Gross, Rabbi Kimberly Herzog Cohen, and Rabbi David Stern (Temple Emanu-El of Dallas)

Kimberly Herzog Cohen and David Stern

Risa Gross

I am of a generation defined by apps and gadgets. Rather than hailing a cab, we Millennials opt to summon an Uber. We rarely touch a newspaper, but our Twitter feed keeps us up to date. We combat our sedentary, screen-focused lifestyle with motivation from our Fitbit. These types of cutting-edge technology are introduced into our lives with almost quotidian frequency, and we are constantly readjusting our patterns and habits to incorporate the newest and the latest. In an era when being the first to have the new iPhone carries prestige, referring to custom or convention smacks of Ludditism. And yet Judaism hearkens back thousands of years in its rituals and practices. What is the value of tradition in a world driven by innovation?

Rabbi Kimberly Herzog Cohen

Risa describes a world driven by "cutting-edge technology," which results in constant flux. Often in the greater culture, new is better. New is attractive. New represents the future and encourages innovation. Risa's concluding question suggests tradition represents the opposite of innovation—something old and stodgy like the

---

KIMBERLY HERZOG COHEN (NY11) is an associate rabbi of Temple Emanu-El of Dallas, TX.

DAVID STERN (NY89) is the senior rabbi of Temple Emanu-El of Dallas, TX, and the President-Elect of the Central Conference of American Rabbis.

faint smell of mildew in a synagogue classroom or the dust that collects on library books.

Tradition is one way we maintain continuity and honor the past. But Judaism has survived and thrived through the centuries because of the innovation that allows tradition to evolve and maintain relevancy. Particularly in our work with Millennials, we must encourage innovation as each generation becomes stakeholders in their Jewish lives. At Temple Emanu-El, in a learning experience designed for couples preparing for marriage, many of our participants are creating interfaith families. Because of their different backgrounds, often these couples have sought guidance for how they can purposefully integrate traditions into their home before they begin the class. And yet we find that both our Jewish-Jewish couples and interfaith couples need encouragement and concrete examples so they can exercise their agency in defining unique traditions together. For example, one couple discovered a way to bring her Catholic Columbian culture into family Chanukah celebrations. It is customary to make fried dough balls, called *bunuelos*, for Christmas in Columbia. Now, they have become their own tasty version of *sufganiyot*! Another couple rediscovered the gift of Shabbat through turning off electronic devices on Saturday mornings and catching up face-to-face while enjoying breakfast on their patio. Although they might choose to observe holidays and Shabbat differently than their parents, these couples are figuring out ways to make Jewish traditions part of their fast-paced lives.

In a world where technology can often place emphasis on individual expression and personal status, we need tradition to help connect us to something greater than ourselves and set our moral compass. Risa describes a world defined by material goods, such as apps and gadgets. While they may inform us of breaking news, count our steps, locate a high school friend, and help us create a to-do list, do these apps and gadgets offer guidance on making hard life decisions? Judaism is rich with stories and rituals that can inspire us to transform the world as part of a network of covenantal relationships. One such story centers on the great teacher, Rabbi Yochanan ben Zakkai. Rabbi Yochanan escaped from the Roman-occupied Jerusalem to establish a new center for learning in the northern city of Yavne. He was a great innovator of tradition, transforming the ancient Temple rituals into Rabbinic Judaism.

Rabbi Yochanan was walking with his student—Rabbi Joshua—near Jerusalem after the destruction of the Temple. Rabbi Joshua looked at the Temple ruins and said: "Alas for us! The place which atoned for the sins of the people Israel through the ritual of animal sacrifice lies in ruins!" Then Rabbi Yochanan spoke to him these words of comfort: "Be not grieved, my son. There is another way of gaining atonement even though the Temple is destroyed. We must now gain atonement through *g'milut chasadim*, acts of loving-kindness, as it is written [in the Book of Hosea]: For I desire *chesed*, not sacrifice" (*Avot D'Rabbi Natan* 11a).

This is a story about one of the most radical changes in Jewish life. Imagine standing before the ruins of the Second Jerusalem Temple, the holy sanctuary dedicated to God that stood for five hundred years, plus the First Jerusalem Temple before it, which also stood for roughly five hundred years. One thousand years of a unique ritual practice and community structure, of identity formation centered around a place where it was believed that Abraham once stood. How could they possibly continue forward? How will the connection between God and the people be sustained? In this pivotal moment when the entire Jewish present faced tremendous upheaval and change, Rabbi Yochanan said, "We must now gain atonement through *g'milut chasadim*, acts of loving-kindness."

Rabbi Yochanan could have said many things to his student but he chose to teach about *g'milut chasadim*. *Chasadim* is the plural form of the Hebrew word *chesed*, which can be translated several ways. *Chesed* is love, loyalty, or loving-kindness, according to the King James Bible. *Chesed* is at the bedrock of covenantal life—the relationships we have with members of our community, with the greater community of which we are a part, and with God. *Chesed* is the action that grows out of these relationships and through which we feel a sense of care, concern, and love for each other.

Every generation needs a meeting place of the spirit, a place where *chesed* can be cultivated, which can occur in synagogue sanctuaries as well as on mountaintops and downtown bars. Mythologist Joseph Campbell writes, "Your sacred space is where you can find yourself again and again." I believe Campbell speaks to an integral part of a synagogue's potential sanctity—the ideal, really, for what a synagogue or any religious place should be. Through shared traditions and rituals, we can discover our inner core and a sense of awe that brings us beyond the ordinary.

The task before conventional Jewish communities, from the small synagogues to the large ones residing in stately buildings that have stood for hundreds of years, is to look broadly at the changes that have already impacted Jewish life as we know it. How can we listen and learn from our Millennials and integrate new ways of engaging spiritual seekers and Jews of all stripes in the richness of our tradition, encouraging innovation as they make their way into adulthood?[1]

Rabbi David Stern

If someone blew [the shofar] in a well, or in a cistern, or in a large barrel, and one heard the sound of the shofar, he has fulfilled his obligation; but if he heard the sound of the echo, he has not fulfilled his obligation. (*Mishnah Rosh HaShanah* 3:7)

Shakespeare's death on April 23, 1616, went largely unremarked by all but a few of his immediate contemporaries . . . Shakespeare's passing was an entirely local English event, and even locally it seems scarcely to have been noted . . . The death of the famous actor Richard Burbage in 1619 excited an immediate and far more widespread outburst of grief. England had clearly lost a great man . . . It was this death that was publicly marked . . . far more than the vanishing of the scribbler who had penned the words that Burbage had so memorably brought alive. (Stephen Greenblatt, "How Shakespeare Lives Now")

Well, which is it? When it comes to innovation, technological or otherwise, is the latest cutting-edge expression of custom and convention a pale echo of the original, like the fragmented sound of a shofar that bounces off the walls of a well, a sound which simply does not count? Or is it a bringing alive of something that is inert until it is enacted in a new way, like the great Burbage animating the words of Shakespeare? Does innovation render tradition irrelevant or magnificent? Is a Torah commentary tweeted out each week a fading note of a once great symphony of complexity and creativity, or is it the medium that brings an ancient message alive?

The answer, of course, is yes. Innovation and tradition desperately need each other. They depend upon each other for mooring, meaning, and humility. Risa asks: "What is the value of tradition in a world driven by innovation?" An answer: they each stand to the other as *eizer k'negdo* (an opposing helpmeet and partner).

It is by now a commonplace to understand that technological innovation presents us with a double-edged sword: the inventions intended to save time and make us more efficient can do the opposite; the gadgets we hope will free us up weigh us down; the same technologies that create a genuine worldwide web of connection can also isolate us from the people before our very eyes.

I have a cousin who was a top executive at Facebook. He took me on a tour of their new campus, and I asked, "How is it that a company whose product is the epitome of the potential for disembodied connection creates a campus so that thousands of people can work in the same place at the same time?" "Because," he said, "there is no replacement for face-to-face encounter."

There is arguably no denying technology's promise and certainly no forestalling its progress. But a good look at the Facebook campus or at the texts of our Musar tradition reminds us that the greatest goods still require limitation and balance. It is both a spiritual and a societal question: How do we optimize the good by grounding it in something greater? Rabbi Harold Schulweis defined idolatry as the category error of mistaking the part for the whole. How do we make sure not to turn the latest technological trend into a dehumanizing idol?

For me, the answer lies in the call for us moderns to stay humble—to recognize that our wondrous technologies are still only means rather than ends and to keep an eye on the spiritual horizons we're striving for in the first place.

That's not easy, and *Mishnah Rosh HaShanah* 3:8 knows the struggle. In it, the Rabbis ask the same question about two important Torah passages. Of the passage in Exodus 17 in which the Israelites prevail whenever Moses lifts his hands, they ask, "But could the hands of Moses wage a battle or lose a battle?" They answer: "This is rather to teach that whenever Israel looked on high and subjected their heart to their [God] in heaven, they prevailed." And of the passage in Numbers 21 in which the Israelites are told that if they look upon the bronze serpent they will be healed of snakebite, the Rabbis ask again, "But could the [bronze] serpent kill or could the [bronze] serpent keep alive?" And they answer: "Only whenever Israel looked on high and subjected their heart to their [God] in heaven were they healed."

Perhaps Moses' hands and the bronze serpent were the Israelites' latest military and medical technologies. Notice that the

Rabbis do not argue with the efficacy of the means, but they want to make sure that we don't confuse the means with the end. They remind us to ground our glance in something greater. In modern terms, they might challenge us to extend our vision beyond the screens in our hands to what those screens point us towards: the human beings at the other end of the communication; the knowledge that can enrich and advance the quality of life; the Torah wisdom that can emerge even from a limited number of characters; via our meditation apps, the Shabbat opportunities for quiet, relationship, healing, and hope.

So back to Risa's question and Kim's enlightened reflection: for me as a Reform Jew, tradition is not an obstruction of vision, not a series of "thou shalt nots" that would suffocate the innovation and creativity that are our calling card. Rather, a la *Rosh HaShanah* 3:8, tradition is an extension of vision—beyond the latest memes and means, towards community both contemporary and historic, and towards the transcendent. So I love both Risa's question and Kim's response—tradition is about self-transcendence and moral compass, authentic relationship and old-new approaches to spiritual practice. How thrilling to consider that new technologies might open access to timeless verities, not as pale echoes, but as ancient wisdom "memorably brought alive": for Millennials and for us all, in each successive generation of questions, answers, and blessing.

Notes

1. I drew inspiration from Rabbi Toba Spitzer's sermon at the following link: http://dorsheitzedek.org/writings/hesed-in-community.

Intergenerational Responsa
Dialogue among Aaron Midler, Rabbi Jeremy Weisblatt, and Rabbi Edwin Goldberg

Jeremy Weisblatt and Edwin Goldberg

Question, Presented by Aaron Midler

I grew up in a household influenced by the Reform Judaism practiced in Connecticut in the 1950s and 1960s. Until my late twenties, I knew very little Hebrew and had a knee-jerk distrust for ritual and tradition. Now in my early thirties, I am embracing a religious life that I had little exposure to as a child (e.g., keeping kosher, attending Saturday Morning Services, counting the Omer), though not because I hear any commandment to do so. Rather, in discovering the various purposes and philosophies that underlie Jewish rituals, and in practicing those rituals, I've uncovered a well of meaning that I did not think existed. I see this experience as one in line with a larger trend in Reform Judaism to reintegrate ritual into religious observance in a way that is quite different from my parents' generation. In the future, what role do you believe ritual observance will play in reconnecting Reform Jews to Judaism, and how do you think Reform Jews will continue to reclaim ritual, if at all? Alternatively, do you see Reform Jews going a different direction altogether in finding meaning in modern lives in a uniquely Jewish way?

Response by Rabbi Jeremy Weisblatt

This *sh'eilah* (question) comes at a time of great transition within the Reform Movement. In the last two decades, our movement has changed with the embracing of people from observant, non-Reform communities, as well as a rediscovered love for and engagement

---

JEREMY WEISBLATT (NY14) is Assistant Rabbi at Temple Sholom, Chicago, IL

EDWIN GOLDBERG (C89) is Senior Rabbi at Temple Sholom, Chicago, IL. He is the author of six books, and co-editor of *Mishkan Hanefesh*, the new Reform Mahzor.

with not only our sacred texts but also the adaptation of mitzvot (commandments) for a Reform context. One need look no further than the Summer 2014 issue of *Reform Jewish Quarterly*, which was devoted to the role of Talmud in Reform Judaism, or to our most recent CCAR publications on sacred practice—from kashrut to expanding liturgical rites within our High Holy Day worship—to see this trend. I believe that Reform Judaism will continue to adapt mitzvot and that this generation will come to find still more guidance offered by our sacred texts (Codes, responsa, etc.). This will be a meaningful partner in the process of defining Reform Judaism for Millennials. Our sacred legal texts help to anchor us in an isolating world that seems to exist without boundaries.

One could simply quote the various articles that seem to indicate that Millennials are drifting farther away from communal affiliation and assume that this indicates a drift away from traditional practice.[1] Yet, as a key study by David Elcott and Stuart Himmelfarb of New York University shows, simply because one is not affiliated with a Jewish institution does not mean that one is disengaged from the Jewish community in other ways.[2] In my experience building a community for Jewish Millennials in Chicago, Jewish life does connect, attract, and engage Millennials if it is presented as accessible, rooted in a flexible view of tradition, and remains socially inclusive.[3]

What does this all mean when we boil down the data and get to the heart of the matter? It means that a significant portion of Millennial Reform and liberal Jews do indeed care about Judaism and its rituals. They care about how these rituals and Judaism are lived and for Reform Judaism to continue to have relevance to their lives as individuals. Correspondingly, our movement needs leaders well-versed in Jewish legal texts and sources to provide guidance and meaning for Millennial Jews. Our leaders need to respond to the needs of our time in a way that is authentically grounded in our tradition. This means we need to continue to develop a Reform halachic practice and cultivate leaders with the ability to transmit this text effectively for Millennials.

As Mark Washofsky writes in his introduction to *Teshuvot for the Nineties*:

> It will not do to argue that we can link ourselves to Jewish religious tradition without the halakhah, that we can substitute other

"friendlier" texts in place of the legal literature . . . [Judaism's] dominant expression is not the search for correct belief but rather a standard of practice that sanctifies us to God's service. And that branch of traditional Jewish literature which most directly concerns practice is the halakhah . . . There is, in other words, no "tradition" of Jewish practice without halakhah. Virtually everything we consider familiar and normative about Jewish life is because of halakhah . . . The list is long. To claim that we are "not halakhic" suggests a groundless, ahistorical Jewish life that does not accurately describe any contemporary Jewish community . . .[4]

This important point—that an effective expression of Judaism needs a halachic practice because halachah is central to the practice of Judaism—is our answer to Aaron's question.

Reform Millennials are seeking authentic norms and guidance for their lives. Though practices will continue to change, and may even look different a generation or two in the future from what we do today, so long as they are based in a fidelity to our halachic heritage, Reform Millennial Jews will represent another strong link in our tradition.

Response by Senior Rabbi Edwin Goldberg

Someone who has never played the piano and starts banging the keys might call it jazz, but it is really just noise. I would extend the metaphor to say that a serious Jewish person, despite the movement to which they adhere, if any, should understand that we take tradition seriously, if not literally.

Since I do not believe that a "supernatural" God commands us, I technically cannot consider myself halachic in observance. Nevertheless, as a practitioner of theological humility—I know that I know little of the world as it truly exists (who does?)—and as a practical pragmatist, I see that the accumulated wisdom of Jewish halachic authorities can help me navigate the difficult questions of life.

To put it another way, I am writing this in a café. I chose to buy and not steal my coffee. Why? Well, there are laws that I respect. Also, I don't want to be arrested. And I don't want to be a person who steals. Any of these reasons guarantee my proper behavior. At this point I am not sure I need worry about which one is the most convincing.

In short, Jewish legal wisdom is often relevant. When it is presented as such, I would not be surprised if younger Jews would be interested in learning about and even following it, despite the theological gap between them and our Sages from millennia ago.

Notes

1. http://www.thejewishweek.com/news/new-york/millennial-study-looks-up-prompts-hands-grants.
2. D. Elcott and S. Himmelfarb, *Generations and Regeneration: Engagement and Fidelity in 21st Century American Jewish Life* (New York: NYU Wagner, The Jewish Boomer Platform, 2014).
3. Numerous articles and news reports detail this and for the sake of brevity for this responsum, I have chosen to cite a few only. Please refer to http://www.thejewishweek.com/news/new-york/millennial-study-looks-up-prompts-hands-grants; http://www.haaretz.com/jewish/features/.premium-1.702963; http://www.chicagobusiness.com/article/20151112/NEWS07/151119935/this-group-wants-jewish-millennials-to-connect-over-food-and-wine; http://labshul.org/high-holidays-for-millennials-but-far-from-shul/7905 among other articles.
4. I am indebted as well to Rabbi Leon Morris for our numerous conversations on the state and future of Reform halachah and halachic practice as well as allowing me to quote from and use his working paper for this article. Leon Morris, "Reforming Reform Judaism," pp. 5, 10, 12–15.

Millennials, Jewish Values, and Climate Change
A Changing Approach to Career and Life

Jason R. Levine and Ruth A. Zlotnick

Part I: Emma Kahle—Millennial Question
Holistic Life/Values Approach to Professional and Personal Lives

In recent generations, there has been a shift in managing the traditional "work-life balance." In our parents' generation, a common approach was to separate the workday from the evening and weekend, when personal values were expressed through extracurricular activities, hobbies, and pursuits. In our generation, more commonly this line between professional work and personal life is blurred, and success is defined through creative and dynamic incorporation of personal values in a professional career. We seek careers that fulfill personal goals and values and approach life holistically, integrating the personal with the professional. How can the inclusion of personal values and beliefs in one's professional career enable Millennial Jews to incorporate elements of their tradition into daily life? In particular, as climate change becomes an increasingly pressing issue in our world, many Millennials will be motivated to respond in a holistic way. How can climate activism reflect the values of Judaism, and how can Judaism strengthen

---

JASON R. LEVINE (C13) is the Associate Rabbi at Temple Beth Am in Seattle, Washington, where he oversees youth engagement within the congregational community.

RUTH A. ZLOTNICK (NY01) is the Senior Rabbi at Temple Beth Am in Seattle, WA, a congregation that prides itself on social justice and engaged and joyous Jewish living. As relative newcomers, she, her husband and their daughter are still in awe of Seattle's majestic natural beauty and are adjusting to the difficulty of finding an excellent New York-style bagel.

their efforts to address this critically important issue in all aspects of their lives?

Part II: Jason Levine—A Millennial Rabbi Response

"Six days you shall labor and do all your work, but the seventh day is a Shabbat of *Adonai* your God [on which] you shall do no work."[1] While God made it clear that work and nonwork have a distinct separation, for the Millennial generation, the boundary is much more transparent.

Emma, I think you are correct that there are thinning and, in many cases, disappearing lines of separation between work and personal life when it comes to how our generation lives out its values. We do not want to check our values at the door just to earn a paycheck, only to then resume our activism, advocacy, or volunteering in the afternoon or weekends when the inbox is unattended.

Millennials have a greater emphasis on why they are at their jobs. *Forbes*'s 2016 list of "The Best Places to Work" concluded: "Ultimately, the companies that perform exceptionally well on this list succeed [by] clearly demonstrating their mission, culture, and values."[2] Furthermore, an April 2016 *Fortune* article highlighted the importance of giving employees time to volunteer: "When employees are actively involved in giving back it can lead to a deeper commitment and connection to the work." They prefer being "actually involved . . . rather than a corporate donation being made."[3] Our generation is not looking for a token gesture regarding our values, but a determined commitment to them.

Your example of climate activism is a model of this holistic approach to Jewish values. After all, our Sages teach that if you are planting a tree and the Messiah appears, you should finish planting the tree before going to greet the Messiah.[4] From this we learn that our values, and environmental values in this case, are meant to be at the forefront of our minds even in the most theologically significant moments. If we are not to cease our work to heal the environment even in the presence of the Messiah, then we most certainly should not be asked to do so at work.

Anecdotally over the past few years, I have asked Millennials, "What issue will your grandchildren look back at you and say, 'How did you let it get this far? Why didn't you do more earlier?'" Almost exclusively, they answer "climate change." For our generation, this is not a political issue or talking point; it is a real-life concern that has implications for our societal and natural future. We want our businesses, homes, schools, and neighborhoods to have a limited carbon footprint, and we emphasize going green as a core value of how we operate in the world.

Our own Reform Movement of Judaism recognizes that climate change is an example of how the younger generation can inspire the older. A 2015 Resolution by the CCAR on Climate Justice declared:

> We may derive hope from polls indicating that America's youngest voters consider the environment to be a much greater priority than do their parents and grandparents. While the CCAR has long recognized this problem and advocated for needed change, we have not made these issues our priority to the extent now being demanded by our youngest colleagues and by young adults in our communities.[5]

Our generation demands that this be a central tenet for our Reform rabbinical organization and movement—and even the entire Jewish people. Millennials assert that we must uphold our values, particularly around climate change, not as an afternoon hobby when the workday ends, but as a necessary and crucial issue for our community throughout all aspects of life, personal and professional.

So what is to be done? In order to be "holistic," we must assert, as you put it, "creative and dynamic incorporation of personal values in a professional career." While your question asked about how individuals can attain this harmony, I believe our most serious work must be done in community. Without a doubt, we must work one-on-one with Millennials within our circles of influence. But, if we hope to support and facilitate a holistic blending of Jewish values for an entire Millennial generation, then our efforts must be greater in scope and have a higher degree of urgency. We need an organizational and philosophical rethinking throughout the Jewish community about how we engage Millennials.

I agree there is a real risk of Millennials disengaging. We are the "spiritual-but-not-religious" generation. We will easily find spiritual fulfillment outside of an organized religious space without grieving the death of the organization that is left behind. The professional Jewish world has, for the most part, failed to recognize that our generation expresses our Jewish identity differently than how many of our institutions are set up to support. We are too busy trying to fit new ideas into old boxes without taking the necessary risks to change not just our calendars, programs, and membership models, but our ways of thinking. It is not enough to create a young adult group at your synagogue or community center; we have to fully understand and adopt a Millennial mentality. If we remain flat-footed and stagnant in understanding how Millennials view their values (Jewish or not) in a holistic way, the game is up.

So instead of digging in our heels with old ideas, let us build anew. Incredible leaders with groundbreaking ideas are trying to reinvent our community in real time. *Slingshot: A Resource Guide to Jewish Innovation* "highlight[s] those organizations in Jewish life with particular resonance among the next generation."[6] It is important to note that many of those leading the most transformative work are from older generations.[7] This challenge is one we can all embrace and be successful.

In conclusion, Emma, while some may claim that the Millennials' disengagement from Jewish community is the death knell of our generation's engagement with Judaism, I argue the reverse, but only if Jewish communities and organizations begin to recognize, understand, and embrace the holistic application of our Jewish values throughout all moments of our lives. Careers need not be the place where our Jewish values are put on hold. Instead, they can become a rich outlet for values-based engagement and offer new connection points for our organized Jewish community, who must continue to evolve as well. We must embrace that values are not hobbies and interests, but necessary for our future survival—such as in the example of climate activism. Millennials are changing the world, Jewish and secular, whether you like it or not, and we want you to join us—and for us to join you.

Part III: Ruth A. Zlotnick—Senior Rabbi Responsum

Perhaps it is a quirk of the rabbinic mind, but as I read your words, Emma and Rabbi Levine, my thoughts also turned to a classic biblical text. The verses that echoed in my mind were not so much a response to the question but rather to the spirit behind your dialogue.

We read in *Kohelet* (Ecclesiastes), "One generation goes, another comes, but the earth remains the same forever . . . there is nothing new beneath the sun!"[8] Your question challenges a literal understanding of this text. Given the rapid destruction of the planet, there *is* something new under the sun—climate change. Tragically, the earth will not remain the same forever. The urgency of the need to address our environmental crisis shakes us to our core and demands our immediate response. The clarion call of your generation is that humanity must change its behavior in order to protect what remains of our earthly home.

However, *Kohelet* articulates an eternal truth: Despite changes in context, the human condition remains the same. Each generation differentiates itself from the ones that precede it, and yet the spectrum of human emotions and the depth of human questions remain the same throughout time.

I came of age during the 1980s, when Reagan was president and yuppies were the rage. These young, well-educated, upwardly mobile urban professionals were considered to be materialistic, self-centered, status-oriented, hard-working, and hard-playing. The yuppie era was the apotheosis of the workday/extra-curricular split described by Emma. The image of the yuppie promulgated in pop culture was elitist—mostly white, socioeconomically privileged, out of touch with the real struggles of most American families.

The truth is, however, that not everyone who graduated college in my generation was oriented toward earning high salaries. Many of us buckled under the yuppie label and sought to live meaningful lives that reflected our values and were socially responsible. And, no doubt, there are members of the Millennial generation who vigorously climb the professional ladder and whose off-hours are devoted to endeavors not appropriate for the workplace. It is easy to overlook the individuals of any demographic cohort who are not at the center of the bell curve.

With that said, Millennials live in a different time than we did, one that has proven to be profoundly precarious. Throughout your lifetime, the status quo has been threatened or overturned by economic crashes, terrorist attacks, and environmental disasters. No wonder your generation redefines success, preferring a deeper integration of your personal values into your professional life. Nothing is more dependable than your own belief system and the relationships you foster in life. And I commend you for it. As *Kohelet* teaches, "Better a poor but wise youth than an old but foolish king who no longer has the sense to heed warnings."[9]

We older folks must heed the Millennial warnings—by supporting your desire to live holistically and enter professional roles that effect social change. Those of us who are older (and therefore more likely to be in positions of leadership) can best serve you by creating work environments that allow for a healthy work/life balance, achieve smaller carbon footprints, and promote justice. Your generation has raised awareness not just about the environmental impact of climate change, but also the socioeconomic impact of our reckless destruction of resources. You have taught us just how much climate activism is intertwined with activism around systemic racism, sexism, and income inequality. The more we see these issues as connected, the better able we will be to remedy them.

We also must heed your warnings regarding institutional Jewish life. The Jewish institutions that served my parents' generation did not generate excitement from my generation; many of my peers also identify as "spiritual but not religious." It's therefore not surprising that Millennials are fully opting out of formal Jewish institutions. We need nothing short of wholesale institutional change for synagogues and other community organizations. We need to innovate ways for people to authentically engage in Jewish learning, prayer, and acts of loving-kindness, and these innovations must attend to the needs of twenty-first-century life. As Rabbi Levine points out, there are already organizations that offer Millennials powerful, relevant, genuine Jewish experiences. Longstanding institutions must support and mirror these efforts.

We need to heed your warnings, but I offer two in return. First, do not mistake the failures of twentieth-century Jewish institutions with failures of Judaism as a system of values and way of life. Through Judaism, individuals can discern their life's purpose, achieving the holistic life balance of which you speak.

Long before we worried about a work/life balance, Judaism offered a pathway for living a values-based life. There is nothing new under the sun. Whether you follow halachah (Jewish law), or derive meaning from contemplative practices such as Musar, or ascribe to Reform Judaism's informed choice, our tradition teaches that everything we do has the ability to draw out the sacred. Jews have lived this way for thousands of years because we recognize "the eye never has enough of seeing nor the ear of hearing."[10] We must make the most of the time we are allotted. This focus on intentional living is not something newly discovered in the twenty-first century.

This brings me to my final word of advice. My fear for you and your peers is that by eschewing organized religion and following your individual path or perhaps participating in your own customized micro-communities, you will deprive yourself of the power and wisdom that comes from engaging in *K'lal Yisrael*, the larger, diverse, multigenerational Jewish community.

Judaism is radically countercultural to the American way of life. Jewish community, when it is vibrant and authentic, makes demands on us that the intense freedom of choice in American society does not. Those ties of kinship, not just with the community today, but with the generations past and yet to be, expands our consciousness and strengthens our character. It cultivates a powerful sense of responsibility toward nurturing all of Creation.

Keep pushing us to be true to our values. It gives me hope, even as we witness the brokenness of our planet and the pain of its inhabitants. Keep teaching us with your wisdom, but please remember: "Wisdom is good with a heritage, and it is a profit to those who see the sun."[11]

Notes

1. Exod. 20:9–10, *The Jewish Bible: Tanakh: The Holy Scriptures*, 1st ed. (Philadelphia: Jewish Publication Society, 1985), adapted by Rabbi Jason Levine.
2. Kathryn Dill, "The Best Places to Work in 2016," *Forbes*, December 14, 2015, http://www.forbes.com/sites/kathryndill/2015/12/14/the-best-places-to-work-in-2016/#e9eaf0c52fe2.
3. Ed Frauenheim and Sarah Lewis-Kullen, "Giving Workers Paid Time Off to Volunteer Will Help Your Company Succeed," *Fortune*, April 26, 2016, http://fortune.com/2016/04/26/giving-workers-paid-time-off-to-volunteer-will-help-your-company-succeed/.
4. *Avot D'Rabbi Natan* 31b, Judah Goldin, trans., *The Fathers According to Rabbi Nathan* (New Haven: Yale University Press, 1990), adapted by Rabbi Jason Levine.
5. "CCAR Resolution on Climate Justice," October 27, 2015, https://ccarnet.org/rabbis-speak/resolutions/2015/ccar-resolution-climate-justice/.
6. "About the Guide," *Slingshot* (2012), http://slingshotfund.org/overview/.

7. Derek Thompson, "The Myth of the Millennial Entrepreneur," *The Atlantic*, July 6, 2016, http://www.theatlantic.com/business/archive/2016/07/the-myth-of-the-millennial-entrepreneur/490058/.
8. Eccles. 1:4, 9, Adele Berlin and Marc Zvi Brettler, eds., *The Jewish Study Bible,* 2nd ed. (Oxford: Oxford University Press, 2014), location 856534, 85673.
9. Eccles. 4:13, ibid., location 85812.
10. Eccles. 1:8, ibid., location 85673.
11. Eccles. 7:1, ibid., location 85890.

Book Reviews

Siddur Lev Shalem: For Shabbat and Festivals
Edward Feld, Senior Editor
(New York: The Rabbinical Assembly, 2016), 466 pp.

Much ink was spilled in December 2013 when Rabbi Daniel Gordis wrote in *The Jewish Review of Books* about the "likely demise" of Conservative Judaism and implied that the movement's end could come within ten years. To the degree that prayer books reflect the vitality of a religious movement, Conservative Judaism's newest offering, *Siddur Lev Shalem: For Shabbat and Festivals*, represents a robust response to Gordis's assertion. The Conservative Judaism of this siddur is filled with a fresh creativity that brings the traditional prayer book to life and into the twenty-first century. *Lev Shalem* represents the next stage of evolution in a Conservative Jewish liturgy that seeks to mediate between tradition on the one hand, and the needs of an eclectic American Jewish community on the other.

Lev Shalem's most significant innovation is the English marginalia on the left-hand pages, and the potential that those passages have to be shared out loud during worship. *Lev Shalem*'s predecessor, *Sim Shalom* (The Rabbinical Assembly, 1985), only has a few passages whose innovative English approaches something of a liturgical *chidush*. For example, as *Sim Shalom*'s editorial team considered the theological diversity of the Conservative Movement at that time, *Sim Shalom* offered a traditional rendition of *K'dushat HaYom* in the *Musaf Amidah* for Shabbat *and* a "Shabbat Alternative Musaf Amidah." The alternative renditions (pp. 446–49 of *Sim Shalom*) contain a choice of four passages (one in Hebrew/English and three just in English) that account for an avoidance or de-emphasis on the sacrificial cult.

There are other creative elements in *Sim Shalom*. (See Yoel Kahn's comments on the three "Who Did Not Make Me . . ." blessings in volume 5 of *My People's Prayer Book* for a thorough review of the Conservative Movement's history with that piece of liturgy, some of which predates *Sim Shalom*.) But regarding the specific role of English in public prayer, it is *Sim Shalom*'s Shabbat Alternative

Musaf Amidah that augurs the Conservative Movement's potential willingness to offer up creative passages solely in English as authentic replacements for long-accepted and established parts of the *matbei-ah t'filah*.

In the thirty years since *Sim Shalom*'s publication, the voices in the Conservative Movement that clamored for more contemporary liturgical choices have only increased. Conservative Judaism, like much of the rest of the American Jewish community, has become more diverse. JTS Chancellor Arnold Eisen speaks directly to that diversity in one of *Lev Shalem*'s introductory pieces:

> *Siddur Lev Shalem* addresses a community more diverse than ever before: men and women familiar with the prayerbook since childhood and adults coming to *t'filah* for the first time, believers in a personal God and believers in a divine force within, or in neither or both. Some will focus on the left-hand pages of translation and reflection. Others will favor the Hebrew text and explanatory notes on the right. All will welcome the generous provision of empty space on the page: an implicit invitation to supplement the words with private meditation and devotion. (p. xxi)

The marginal notes that Eisen refers to are the most remarkable aspect of this siddur. Many of the passages would be welcome additions to our own worship and easily call to mind the diverse poetic voices of our *Mishkan T'filah*.

On the creative contributions on the left-hand margins, Edward Feld notes:

> In the left-hand column are insights fostered by medieval and contemporary prose and poetry that reflect on some of the themes of the prayer on that page. Sometimes these selections expand on the theme of the prayer; sometimes they are in dialogue with the text, querying its presuppositions, offering alternative ways of understanding the issue at hand. In keeping with the tradition of the siddur as an anthology of Jewish thought, these selections draw from the full compass of Jewish writing . . . In sum, they provide models of how we might make the moment of prayer our own, a source of spiritual nourishment. (pp. xiii–xiv)

It is too early to say how our Conservative friends will use the English passages in their worship. Will their inclusion in this siddur herald the beginning of a trend for increased creativity and

English in their *t'filot*? Or will the passages be a silent commentary that worshipers can encounter on their own, to do with as they would? Regardless, for our own Reform prayer, *Lev Shalem* is a remarkable and valuable supplement to *Mishkan T'filah* and the worship that so many of us are called upon to facilitate. *Lev Shalem* most certainly deserves a spot in the liturgical section of our rabbinic libraries for us to consult as we do that sacred work.

JEFFREY BROWN (C05), Rabbi of Scarsdale Synagogue Temples Tremont and Emanu-El, Scarsdale, NY.

Eight Questions of Faith: Biblical Challenges that Guide and Ground Our Lives
Niles Elliot Goldstein
(Philadelphia: Jewish Publication Society, 2015), 188 pp.

As a matter of disclosure I have known Rabbi Goldstein for a long time. His parents are members of my former congregation, and Niles and I edited a book together. I am one of his admirers and have read most of the ten books he has written. His latest book, *Eight Questions of Faith: Biblical Challenges That Guide and Ground Our Lives*, is a powerful and learned exploration of eight questions that each of us faces at some moment in our lives:

1. How do we live when we know we are going to die?
2. Why is humility so important?
3. Are we responsible for other people?
4. What is the purpose of human life?
5. Is some knowledge too dangerous to possess?
6. Has God abandoned us?
7. How do we return when we have lost our way?
8. What happens to us after we die? (p. xiv)

We are told if we are going to write a book we should write about something we know. This book as well as his other books is autobiographical. The questions emerge from his reflection on his own experience, his own life, and his extensive study of Judaism as well as literature, philosophy, and theology. There is a brutal honesty that pervades his writing. He is a fierce critic of what he perceives to be wrong in the Jewish world, and he is no less brutally honest about himself. His writing style allows the reader to feel his emotions and connect directly with the existential questions that haunt every thinking human being. The book does not provide answers to the questions he poses, but using his own life and material drawn from a broad range of sources both Jewish and non-Jewish, he offers guidance for individuals to seek their own answers. *Eight Questions* is not a work of academic scholarship but it demonstrates Niles's deep understanding of complex and diverse material drawn from his ever-growing pursuit of wisdom wherever it may be found. It should be clear that this is not a self-help book but a work of literature that seeks to confront the crises each person confronts at various stages of their lives.

Each chapter begins with a vivid description of an event in his life that presented him with a fundamental dilemma. His descriptions of his own pain and angst are starkly compelling. The reader is drawn into his life and through the words on the page feels present with Niles as he confronts one crisis after another. In each instance the reader wonders how Niles will resolve the crisis and find the ability to utilize the crisis to find the wisdom that enables him to continue his journey. After describing each crisis Niles turns to a biblical verse to begin his ruminations. Niles's choice of a biblical verse reminds the reader that what Niles is experiencing has been experienced before. These are the eternal questions. His own struggle is unique in that it comes out of his own autobiography, but it is not unique because other people before and after have and will in their own way ask the same question that is raised by the biblical verse. The book therefore belongs to a genre of literature that asks the reader not to read the *Tanach* as an ancient artifact but to read it as the story of his/her own life.

In chapter 1 Niles tells the reader that his despair had become so profound that he contemplated flinging himself off a cliff into the churning waters below. Instead of suicide he chose life. When your life is falling apart to whom do you turn? Niles turns to the prophet Jeremiah who cries out in despair, "Why did I ever issue from the womb?" (Jer. 20:18). Niles explores Jeremiah's dark despair then turns to *Kohelet*, then to the poet Shelly, then to the philosophers Franz Rosenzweig and Maimonides, then to the artist Paul Gauguin, then to the *Mishnah Pirkei Avot*, then to Shakespeare's Hamlet, and finally to Samuel Beckett. Each chapter has a broad range of sources. At the end of the chapter Niles writes, "When all seems lost, when the burden of our story seems too great for us to bear, our ungraspable drive to endure has the power to carry, preserve, and ultimately rescue us" (p. 25). The chapter as with the book as a whole has intellectual and emotional integrity. The goal is not to talk a potential suicide off the cliff but to help the reader to find a way to contextualize his/her struggles with the wisdom gained from the struggles of some of the giants of the Bible, philosophy, and literature. Niles uses texts to speak to himself, with himself, and for himself in the hope that others will be drawn into his personal conversation and it will become his/her conversation as well.

In chapter 2 Niles's encounter with nature becomes an experience of the transcendent that leads him to Moses' response to God at the Burning Bush, "Who am I that I should go to Pharaoh?" (Exod. 3:11). He explores the concept of humility. Moses' own sense of unworthiness and his fear and trembling are the starting point of his ability to accept God's charge. Niles describes Moses' reaction as "radical humility." Strength and courage can come from humility. The chapter challenges the reader to contemplate how at every stage of life there are opportunities for growth. The theme is that in self-diminution there is the potential for greatness. As Moses faces Pharaoh, so each of us is called to face the Pharaohs and the *Mitzrayim* the narrow constricting moments in our lives.

In chapter 3 Niles offers a new way of looking at Cain's famous question, "Am I my brother's keeper?" (Gen. 4:9). His is a refreshing and creative take on what many perceive as a simple question or perhaps a simple accusation by God. At this early stage of creation why should one assume that Cain would know the correct response? Perhaps God bears some of the moral burden? How do human beings develop a moral conscience? For me this was the most interesting and creative interpretation of the age-old, well-known story.

Chapter 4 deals with the concept of being called. Beginning with his own decision to become a rabbi, Niles turns to a quotation from Deuteronomy:

> And now, O Israel, what does the LORD your God demand of you? Only this: to fear the LORD your God, to walk only in His paths, to love Him, and to serve the LORD your God with all your heart and soul, keeping the LORD's commandments and laws, which I enjoin upon you today, for your good. (Deut. 10:12–13)

He does not parse all elements of the demands but turns his attention to the demand to fear God. The chapter is about a quest to find meaning and purpose in one's life. He ends the chapter by returning to the question "What does God demand of you?," concluding that God demands "an open heart. And a brave soul" (p. 85). In this chapter, as in the others, the journey to conclusion is provocative and profound. He draws constantly on diverse sources.

Chapter 5 deals with Adam and Eve's eating of the forbidden fruit and God's question "What have you done?" (Gen. 3:13). Niles explores the question of whether there is knowledge that humankind should not pursue because it is too dangerous. His conclusion seems to be yes but he reminds the reader that "Forbidden knowledge is as dangerous as it is seductive" (p. 98) and for that reason the reality is that humans will always seek to know more without necessarily understanding the potential consequences. Since one cannot stop the pursuit of knowledge, humankind needs to develop an ethics of anticipation. Niles provides a stark warning and a necessary caution. The final words of the chapter are, "In the end, we take our chances whenever we embark on the pursuit of knowledge, since we can never be fully certain where our discoveries will take us. Whether our actions result in a revelation of light or a disclosure of darkness is not ultimately in our hands" (p. 106). This is true but it does not mean that humans should not seek to control the uses to which knowledge is applied.

In chapter 6 he utilizes Psalms 22:2, "My God, my God why have You abandoned me?," to describe the apparent absence of God at crucial moments in history or in one's life. How does one cross the abyss? Intellectualizing alone does not alleviate the profound loneliness nor fill the void. However he discovers in profound encounters with others something powerful can happen. Engagement with others is a path to one's own spirituality.

In chapter 7 Malachi's question "How shall we return?" (3:7) concerns one's sense of being lost and finding the correct path to return home. Niles explores the concept of *t'shuvah* as journey. After exploring the concept in Jewish sources he turns to Homer and Coleridge. Tying diverse sources together gives a universal dimension to the book. Niles takes the reader on an unexpected journey. In this chapter he offers the notion that returning home is not necessarily going to a place where one once was but a place where one will arrive to renew one's life.

BOOK REVIEWS

Chapter 8 begins with Job's question "If a man dies, can he live again?" (14:14). It is an exploration of life after death. There is physical death and there is spiritual death that occurs while one is still living. Rebirth can be a reality in the face of spiritual death but what about in the face of physical death? In one of the most provocative lines in the book, Niles writes, "If rebirth and resurrection are possible in this world, why is it far-fetched to imagine they will be possible in the world-to-come?" (p. 161).

This is an important book. Individuals will profit from reading *Eight Questions of Faith*. There is much wisdom to be gained from Niles's thought process and uses of sources. His combination of autobiography and textual analysis is a model that allows the wisdom of texts to interact with the realities of living. His writing style is engaging. Niles has a gift of taking one to the place where he is, physically and emotionally. His thinking offers wonderful insights into how one can process his/her existential dilemmas. As much pleasure as I had from reading the book alone, I can imagine how much more rewarding it would be reading together with others in an adult study class or a men's book group. The book is a genuine contribution to contemporary explorations of the intersection of Judaism and real life issues that every person faces.

PETER KNOBEL, PhD. (C69), Rabbi Emeritus of Beth Emet, the Free Synagogue, Evanston, IL, and former President of the CCAR.

Call for Papers: *Maayanot*

The CCAR Journal: The Reform Jewish Quarterly is committed to serving its readers' professional, intellectual, and spiritual needs. In pursuit of that objective, the *Journal* created a new section known as *Maayanot* (Primary Sources), which made its debut in the Spring 2012 issue.

We continue to welcome proposals for *Maayanot* —translations of significant Jewish texts, accompanied by an introduction as well as annotations and/or commentary. *Maayanot* aims to present fresh approaches to materials from any period of Jewish life, including but not confined to the biblical or Rabbinic periods. When appropriate, it is possible to include the original document in the published presentation.

Please submit proposals, inquiries, and questions to *Maayanot* editor, Daniel Polish, dpolish@optonline.net.

Along with submissions for *Maayanot*, the *Journal* encourages the submission of scholarly articles in fields of Jewish Studies, as well as other articles that fit within our Statement of Purpose.

The *CCAR Journal: The Reform Jewish Quarterly*
Published quarterly by the Central Conference of American Rabbis.

Volume LXIV, No. 1. Issue Number: Two hundred fifty-one

Winter 2017

STATEMENT OF PURPOSE

The *CCAR Journal: The Reform Jewish Quarterly* seeks to explore ideas and issues of Judaism and Jewish life, primarily—but not exclusively—from a Reform Jewish perspective. To fulfill this objective, the Journal is designed to:

1. provide a forum to reflect the thinking of informed and concerned individuals—especially Reform rabbis—on issues of consequence to the Jewish people and the Reform Movement;

2. increase awareness of developments taking place in fields of Jewish scholarship and the practical rabbinate, and to make additional contributions to these areas of study;

3. encourage creative and innovative approaches to Jewish thought and practice, based upon a thorough understanding of the traditional sources.

The views expressed in the Journal do not necessarily reflect the position of the Editorial Board or the Central Conference of American Rabbis.

The *CCAR Journal: The Reform Jewish Quarterly* (ISSN 1058-8760) is published quarterly by the Central Conference of American Rabbis, 355 Lexington Avenue, 18th Floor, New York, NY, 10017. Application to mail at periodical postage rates is pending at New York, NY and at additional mailing offices.

Subscriptions should be sent to CCAR Executive Offices, 355 Lexington Avenue, 18th Floor, New York, NY, 10017. Subscription rate as set by the Conference is $100 for a one-year subscription, $150 for a two-year subscription. Overseas subscribers should add $36 per year for postage. POSTMASTER: Please send address changes to CCAR Journal: The Reform Jewish Quarterly, c/o Central Conference of American Rabbis, 355 Lexington Avenue, 18th Floor, New York, NY, 10017.

Typesetting and publishing services provided by Publishing Synthesis, Ltd., 39 Crosby Street, New York, NY, 10013.

The *CCAR Journal: The Reform Jewish Quarterly* is indexed in the *Index to Jewish Periodicals*. Articles appearing in it are listed in the *Index of Articles on Jewish Studies* (of *Kirjath Sepher*).

© Copyright 2017 by the Central Conference of American Rabbis.
All rights reserved.
ISSN 1058-8760

ISBN: 978-0-88123-284-4

GUIDELINES FOR SUBMITTING MATERIAL

1. The *CCAR Journal* welcomes submissions that fulfill its Statement of Purpose whatever the author's background or identification. Inquiries regarding publishing in the CCAR Journal and submissions for possible publication (including poetry) should be sent to the editor, Rabbi Paul Golomb, journaleditor@ccarnet.org.

2. Other than commissioned articles, submissions to the *CCAR Journal* are sent out to a member of the editorial board for anonymous peer review. Thus submitted articles and poems should be sent to the editor with the author's name omitted. Please use MS Word format for the attachment. The message itself should contain the author's name, phone number, and e-mail address, as well as the submission's title and a 1–2 sentence bio.

3. Books for review and inquiries regarding submitting a review should be sent directly to the book review editor, Rabbi Evan Moffic, at *emoffic@gmail.com*.

4. Inquiries concerning, or submissions for, *Maayanot* (Primary Sources) should be directed to the *Maayanot* editor, Rabbi Daniel Polish, at *dpolish@optonline.net*.

5. Based on Reform Judaism's commitment to egalitarianism, we request that articles be written in gender-inclusive language.

6. The *Journal* publishes reference notes at the end of articles, but submissions are easier to review when notes come at the bottom of each page. If possible, keep this in mind when submitting an article. Notes should conform to the following style:
   a. Norman Lamm, *The Shema: Spirituality and Law in Judaism* (Philadelphia: Jewish Publication Society, 1998), 101–6. **[book]**
   b. Lawrence A. Hoffman, "The Liturgical Message," in *Gates of Understanding*, ed. Lawrence A.Hoffman (New York: CCAR Press, 1977), 147–48, 162–63. **[chapter in a book]**
   c. Richard Levy, "The God Puzzle," *Reform Judaism* 28 (Spring 2000): 18–22. **[article in a periodical]**
   d. Lamm, *Shema*, 102. **[short form for subsequent reference]**
   e. Levy, "God Puzzle," 20. **[short form for subsequent reference]**
   f. Ibid., 21. **[short form for subsequent reference]**

7. If Hebrew script is used, please include an English translation. If transliteration is used, follow the guidelines abbreviated below and included more fully in the **Master Style Sheet**, available on the CCAR website at *www.ccarnet.org*:

   "ch" for *chet* and *chaf* "ei" for *tzeirei*

   "f" for *fei* "a" for *patach* and *kamatz*

   "k" for *kaf* and *kuf* "o" for *cholam* and *kamatz katan*

   "tz" for *tzadi* "u" for *shuruk* and *kibbutz*

   "i" for *chirik* "ai" for *patach* with *yod*

   "e" for *segol*

   Final "h" for final *hei*; none for final *ayin* (with exceptions based on common usage): *atah, Sh'ma,* <u>but</u> *Moshe*.

   Apostrophe for *sh'va nah*: *b'nei, b'rit, Sh'ma*; no apostrophe for *sh'va nach*.

   Hyphen for two vowels together where necessary for correct pronunciation: *ne-eman, samei-ach,* <u>but</u> *maariv*, Shavuot.

   No hyphen for prefixes unless necessary for correct pronunciation: *babayit*, HaShem, Yom HaAtzma-ut.

   Do not double consonants (with exceptions based on dictionary spelling or common usage): *t'filah, chayim,* <u>but</u> *tikkun*, Sukkot.

www.ingramcontent.com/pod-product-compliance
Lightning Source LLC
Chambersburg PA
CBHW070403240426
43661CB00056B/2520